D0892123

David Stancliffe has been Bishop of Salisbury since 1993. Before that he was Provost of Portsmouth at a period when the cathedral's worship and ministry were being developed and the cathedral building completed and reordered. Previously he had experience as a curate in Leeds, as a school chaplain and as Director of Ordinands. Bishop Stancliffe has been a member of the Liturgical Commission since 1986 and its chairman since 1993. He is a practising musician, chairman of the editorial panel of *Celebrating Common Prayer* and author of *The Pilgrim Prayerbook*.

To David and Jon
with thanks for
a wonderful break
in Mull
Peter

Lent 2004

God's Pattern

Shaping Our Worship, Ministry and Life

David Stancliffe

First published in Great Britain in 2003 by
Society for Promoting Christian Knowledge
Holy Trinity Church
Marylebone Road
London NW1 4DU

Copyright © David Stancliffe 2003

All rights reserved. No part of this book may be reproduced or transmitted
in any form or by any means, electronic or mechanical, including
photocopying, recording, or by any information storage and retrieval
system, without permission in writing from the publisher.

Extracts from *Common Worship: Services and Prayers for the Church of England*
are copyright © The Archbishops' Council, 2000 and are reproduced by
permission.

Extracts from The Book of Common Prayer, the rights in which are vested
in the Crown, are reproduced by permission of the Crown's Patentee,
Cambridge University Press.

Scripture quotations, unless otherwise noted, are the author's own translation.
Extracts (marked AV) from the Authorized Version of the Bible (The King
James Bible), the rights in which are vested in the Crown, are reproduced by
permission of the Crown's Patentee, Cambridge University Press.
Scripture quotations (marked NIV) are taken from the HOLY BIBLE, NEW
INTERNATIONAL VERSION. Copyright © 1973, 1978, 1984 by International
Bible Society. Used by permission of Hodder & Stoughton Ltd, a member of
the Hodder Headline Plc Group.
Scripture quotations marked RSV are from the Revised Standard Version of the
Bible, copyright © 1946, 1952 and 1971 by the Division of Christian
Education of the National Council of the Churches of Christ in the USA.
Used by permission. All rights reserved.

British Library Cataloguing-in-Publication Data
A catalogue record for this book is available from the British Library

ISBN 0-281-05360-X

10 9 8 7 6 5 4 3 2 1

Designed and typeset by Kenneth Burnley, Wirral, Cheshire
Printed in Great Britain by the Cromwell Press

'Now I know why the churches are true,' said a four-year-old watching a televised service from one of our cathedrals: 'The people in them enjoy singing, and walk about in patterns.'

HOW THE EMMAUS
STORY UNFOLDS . . .

HEARING GOD'S STORY

TELLING OUR STORY

EMBRACE US THE SHAPE OF WORSHIP

LETTING THE SHAPE OF WORSHIP

THE FIRE OF PENTECOST CHANGES US

THE LOVE OF GOD TRANSFORMS THE WORLD

BECOMING DISCIPLES

CELEBRATING CHANGE

FOLLOWING OUR CALLING

TRANSFORMING RELATIONSHIPS
dm

. . . INTO THE EASTER
PATTERN OF LIVING NOW

Contents

Foreword

What is most refreshing about this very refreshing book is Bishop David's clarity about the fact that Christianity is life before it is system. To learn to be a Christian is a lot more like learning to swim than learning the periodic table of the elements or French irregular verbs. When you have begun to learn to swim, you will find all sorts of things to say, right and wrong ways of talking and acting – but the plunge into the water comes first.

Bishop David writes, quite literally, about this plunge into the water. Baptism comes first; and as we work out what it means to swim in the baptismal waters of Christ's risen life, we come to understand a bit more who Christ is and what we must say about him. And we learn how to give our lives the rhythm they need to keep moving through the water – rhythms of personal discipline and prayer, rhythms of Bible reading and sacraments.

This enormously readable and attractive book offers new perspectives on all sorts of things, from the importance of singing to the theology of ordained ministry. It is a fine refresher course for any Christian, and a very good book to put into the hands of anyone who wonders what sort of difference it makes to your life to be a baptized believer. Vivid analogies abound, unexpected insights on familiar things and stories; we are introduced into a wonderfully large and abundant world. Here is Christian faith and practice presented not as a scheme or rule to follow but as, simply, life in the new creation.

ROWAN WILLIAMS

Preface

This book is for those who have tumbled to the fact that they are baptized and want to do something about it. They may be exploring their gifts and trying to see how God wants to use them. They may be trying to make sense of what God is doing in their daily living alongside their pattern of prayer and worship. How do these connect? They may be trying to forge a spirituality that has an intellectual integrity rather than one which offers those kind of golden dreams that vanish at the first challenge from an apparently inhospitable culture. They may be ordained or lay, but they will be restless spirits, wanting to explore what God is doing and how they can be part of it.

The Genesis of this book has, like its biblical namesake, two creation stories with distinct but complementary approaches. One creation story is about my own experience of learning again how to minister over the ten years or so since coming to Salisbury, and tries to give some theological shape to what I have found myself doing, how my convictions have been clarified and what I want to share with others about what I have learnt. The people I most have to thank for this – and Chapter 1 tells some of the story – are the clergy and people of the diocese, and by extension our partners in the Province of the Sudan who are such a key part of our life in Salisbury. Learning how to listen to and respond to their needs has shaped the way I now more consciously try to minister, as will become clear.

The other creation story is more personal. I have tried over the years I have been ordained to find a simple framework that would undergird what I believed about my relationship with God and what it meant. The Christian faith, as expressed doctrinally, seems so complicated. And how do doctrine and life cohere? Can I reduce these complicated ideas to a simple formula that I can share with a sixth-former or a Dorset churchwarden in a way that will help them shape their lives according to the way of Christ? In this personal quest I read many books, pondered long and tried to work it out – as most clergy do – in carefully crafted sermons; but not to much effect. So it was a great surprise when a close colleague said to me, 'Have you never realized that you are the kind of person who does their thinking with other people?'

As a matter of fact, I hadn't. I'd always been brought up with the idea that thinking was something you did on your own, and it was quite a surprise to reckon that it might be in the to-and-fro of conversation that a person like me forges and tests their ideas. But I should have known better. It is, after all, in the direct encounter with the living Word that God engages with us and changes us. After some millennia of making covenants, giving commandments and sending messages via prophets, God finally – 'in these latter days', as the opening verses of the Letter to the Hebrews puts it – decided that there was nothing for it but to come and talk face to face. Personal encounter, not distant commands, is what engages people and changes hearts and minds. So in these latter years I have been trying to do it better.

If that was the Genesis, then the Exodus – the active push – came from an old friend, Ruth McCurry. For some time, people had been trying to persuade me to write something about these convictions. But there was no time, and anyway, I said, there are more than enough books in the world already. But I was persuaded to have some conversations with Ruth that we would tape and have transcribed so that we could work on them and see if they proved interesting. It sounded fairly painless at the time, though of course there has turned out to have been more to it than that. But it may help explain why what follows is not deathless, pellucid theological prose of the kind you might expect bishops to write, but an essentially circular set of reflections on a central theme, still sounding – I am told – like me speaking. Ruth has done an amazing job on the book, and so has Diana, my long-suffering secretary, who when told I was going to write a book in my spare moments last year, said as directly as always, 'You can't, and you won't!' But even if I'm not at all sure that I can, I have, though it's not a conventional book, as Clare Hurst, who typed out all the tapes so laboriously, knows well.

If that has been the Genesis and the Exodus, then the Leviticus, the work of the professional worship-makers, has made an important contribution to my life for a long time. Much of this book is shot through with my reflections on how we can approach worship with the expectation that something might actually happen there, that we might come face to face with God and be changed (though if you shared that expectation with many of those who go regularly to church, I sometimes suspect that they might not go at all!). I mind a lot about worship, and wonder at the quality of what is offered in some places in this most important area of the Church's life. In an age when the standards of public performance are so high, how do worshippers manage to keep on going to church faithfully when the way worship is prepared and offered is often so dire; when it is frequently confused with entertainment, and when it is led by those who apparently have no idea about what they are doing or professional competence in doing it? As for the liturgy itself, I am not a professional liturgist, but have been lucky enough to have many highly skilled colleagues in that world among my friends. I owe an enormous amount of my formation to them; the Liturgical Commission has been a stimulating part of my continuing ministerial education for nearly twenty years and its theological discussions second to none. I hope all its members, past as well as present, know how important they are to me.

As for Numbers, the view of the Promised Land is always tantalizing, but – like other glimpses of the future – can lead to unreal expectations. The book of Numbers chronicles repeated journeys that kept the people of Israel going round in circles for more than a generation. Moses never reached the Promised Land, and I might well have continued circling round these themes but for the discipline imposed by having to order my thoughts that writing this down provided. Grappling with the realities and not endlessly living with intriguing possibilities is what my wife, Sarah, is so good at. She is both practised and skilled at drawing me into a degree of realism, helping me to live in the present moment, for which I am deeply grateful. She knows that mission is about how to live in our here and now in a faithful walking with God and not in hankering after a romantic past or dreaming of an unrealizable future. It is the quality of our life together in the Christian community as we circle the wilderness that shapes us into the kind of people who might have the nerve to take on the cities of the plain.

In this book, some of these little detours or circular excursions appear like this in the text: if you want to get there quickly, you can leave them out. I enjoy that kind of thing, but in the end, you have to get organized and go for it if you are going to have a shot at entering the Promised Land.

Finally, let me try to be concise about the Deuteronomy, my attempt to represent my underlying convictions. My conviction is that what is most important about the Christian life is the quality of our relationships – with God and with one another. It is not so much the fact that we have these relationships, that we do relate; it is more about *how* we relate, and *how* those relationships develop. What matters to me – and I believe to God – are the verbs and adverbs, not the substantives. Being interested in the substantives (things and how they are constructed), rather than the verbs and adverbs (how things relate), is akin to another modern heresy. There's a doctrine abroad that believes in salvation by knowledge. Our huge dependence on the Internet is a case in point. But knowledge about something or someone and knowing them are two quite different things. You may know a lot about Iraq, but that is quite different from knowing Iraqis. 'Sir, we would see Jesus' is what the crowds asked Philip.

Nor is this just a battle between Church and secular culture. I watch other Christian traditions build systematic theologies: defining our relationship to God in words, and then using these verbal formulas as building blocks to create definitions and proofs to construct the whole logical edifice of belief. But I don't think that's how most people experience faith. For them, the truth of the Christian faith is personal, not propositional. They believe because they are attracted to Jesus; he draws them, and he draws them out of themselves into a broader world, and they find that liberating and exciting. It makes them walk tall.

The pursuit of the personal rather than the propositional is quintessentially Anglican. To do theology relationally, to replace dogmatic constructions with relationships, is to take a risk. But it doesn't mean that we are into relativism: it means recognizing that truth is not propositional but personal. In John's Gospel, Jesus says, 'I am the Way, the Truth and the Life.' He does not offer a system but an invitation. We are not won by logic: we make for what is attractive, what draws us, for a relationship that promises a reciprocity. Our question is not so much, 'Is it correct?' but, 'Is it beautiful?'

It was beauty that transfixed Prince Vladimir's emissaries when they experienced the liturgy in Hagia Sophia, the great church of the Holy Wisdom in Constantinople:

> We knew not whether we were in heaven or on earth. For on earth there is no such splendour or such beauty, and we are at a loss how to describe it. We know only that God dwells there among men, and their service is fairer than the ceremonies of other nations. For we cannot forget that beauty.

And it was beauty that won St Augustine, who wrote:

> Late have I loved Thee, O Beauty both so ancient and so new,
> yea, too late I came to love thee;
> for behold, Thou wert within me, and I outside;
> and I sought Thee outside
> and in my unloveliness fell upon those lovely things that Thou
>   hast made.
> Thou wert with me, and I was not with Thee.
> I was kept from Thee by those things,
> yet had they not been in Thee, they would have not been at all.
> Thou didst call and cry to me to break open my deafness;
> Thou didst send forth thy beams
> and shine upon me and chase away my blindness.
> Thou didst breathe fragrance upon me,
> and I drew in my breath and do now pant for Thee.
> I tasted Thee, and now hunger and thirst for Thee;
> Thou didst touch me, and I ever burn again to enjoy Thy peace.

Acknowledgements

On p. 170, the extract from Janet Morley, 'As a woman in labour' in *All Desires Known* (SPCK, 1992) has been altered with the kind permission of the author.

On p. 159, the extracts from Dag Hammarskjöld, *Markings* (Faber and Faber, 1964) have been reproduced by kind permission of the publisher.

Every effort has been made to trace and acknowledge copyright holders of material reproduced in this book. The publisher apologizes for any errors that might remain and, if notified, will ensure that full acknowledgements are made in a subsequent edition.

1 | Discovering God's Pattern

Stepping into a new world

When we step forward into a new world in our journey through life – for example, to a new job, or a new place, or a new relationship – there is an enormous amount to be learnt. It is very rare for someone to embark on a new job or a new role in life knowing exactly what needs to be done and how to do it, without the need to learn about the past history and the geography, the setting, the resources, the possibilities, the hopes and the failures.

A map of some kind may be the first thing you need. Maps show how bits relate together and help you understand how you get from A to B, because they show you how A and B relate – is there a valley, river or hill in between? Is what looks like the most direct route the best; and does best mean the most interesting or the quickest? There are natural patterns of relationship between communities and natural geographical divisions, and in Dorset and Wiltshire, where I live and work, some of the natural geographical features are very significant, like the great mass of Salisbury Plain. On the rolling downland west of Salisbury, the old drove roads ran straight along the top of the hills; down in the bottom of the valleys the roads are narrower and have sudden kinks that show they have grown from the footpaths that once followed the edges of the fields and linked holding to holding and hamlet to hamlet.

When you meet people as you journey about the world, what do you want to know? What do you ask them? The two basic questions are, 'Where have you come from?' and 'Where are you going?'; and on the whole people find it easier to tell you where they have come from. That's in their recent experience, and they have a clear picture of that place and some sense of belonging to it. But it's much more difficult to describe where it is that you are going. You may not know what it looks like, so how will you know when you have arrived?

The idea of a journey to a new and unknown place was the theme of *Pilgrim's Progress*, John Bunyan's popular spiritual classic, and has been a continuing thread through all the pilgrimages that people have made down the centuries. Over the past decade or so, the journey has re-emerged as a model or pattern for the Christian life. When I had a sabbatical some years ago, Sarah and I set off to walk to Compostela in Spain, the shrine of St James and the most popular of all the European pilgrimage destinations in the Middle Ages when Jerusalem was barred to Westerners. In France, the pilgrimage routes are well marked by flashes, and the route is one of those carefully mapped Grandes Randonnées, so it is difficult to lose your way entirely. But when we reached Spain, maps became more difficult to find, and much of the time we found ourselves walking blind, unable to tell how the land ahead lay, and when we might get to what stopping place for the night. For six weeks we hardly read a thing: our heads were full of the changing landscape and of the conversations we had with our fellow pilgrims. Some we only met for one evening, as we shared a hostel dormitory; others we walked alongside for days, until finally either we or they walked just that bit further one day, so fell into company with another little group. On the way, people told each other their stories and asked the questions they had come on this journey to resolve: 'Should we get married?', 'Should I seek profession as a nun?', 'Now I've retired, what should I give the rest of my life to?'

We live our lives at a time of swift change. We are constantly on the move, and coping with change is most people's major preoccupation. The Christian faith should help us here: the heart of the faith is about change, the change that God offers us and longs to see in us and in everyone. So most people find the image of life as an unfolding journey helpful, and it is natural to think of our Church as a place where you weave people that you meet into the continuing journey. The journey is going, so the Church hopes and believes, to God. We get there because by baptism we are incorporated into Christ, and drawn up in him to the Father. And we don't walk alone; people have trodden the way before us and blazed the trail – that's the role of the saints – and we catch our hand into the hand of the person in front and get swept up into this great conga or chain. In the journey that each person takes in life, we all hope to end up somewhere else from where we started.

In a new context

So particularly when we move into a new context – it may be moving to a new parish if you are a parish priest or into a new job if you are a lay person; it may be moving into a new phase of life, like college or retirement, or into a new relationship – what you need is some kind of map so that you can see where you are in relation to the landmarks around you. You also need a purpose, a sense of direction, which is founded on an understanding of where you are, what resources you have, and where you are going. We all need this sense of direction, whether we are bishops, parish clergy or lay people, in contributing to the decisions about the shape, purpose and direction of our diocese or parish, our jobs and lives.

A wide range of opportunities

A new parish priest, and a new bishop equally, is faced by a wide range of opportunities and expectations. When I found myself appointed Bishop here in Salisbury, I discovered that there was no training course available for new bishops for some 18 months, and a professional head-hunter kindly gave me some self-awareness and relationship training. Then I plunged in. My first decision was to go and introduce myself to the clergy, and to get to know something of a large diocese that felt quite diffuse in comparison with the one I'd come from. In origin, that was a largely pragmatic decision. I had come in close on the heels of my predecessor, and as well as work needing to be done on the house, my hunch was that there should be some pause for breath before I started.

So I set out to introduce myself to the clergy of the diocese: to see what they wanted to tell me and to listen to what they had to offer. It took nearly four months: I saw all the clergy (except for those in curacy posts) between Epiphany and Palm Sunday, meeting six or seven a day. The pattern was to go and meet each priest and have the best part of an hour in their study, with them telling me whatever they wanted about themselves, and me sharing some of my enthusiasms and prejudices too. We would then walk to the nearest of their churches, perhaps meeting the churchwardens if they were free, and praying together briefly before I went on to the next one. During these visits, we stayed locally, and one of the archdeacons kindly lent us a caravan which served as a kind of travelling wardrobe and study.

Ministry together

I asked only one direct question during those visits, which was, 'What are you going to give me for my ministry?' It was a question that met with an almost total blank. Many clergy were taken by surprise, as most people's assumption is that bishops are there not to receive but to dish out, and that somehow by being consecrated a bishop one would become elderly, courteous, wise and reserved and have all the right answers to everything. In addition to their natural wariness about a new bishop, the idea that you might actually want to work with your fellow clergy, and indeed need a lot from them, was miles from their expectations. So I got very few direct answers to my question. Indeed, I suspect that quite a lot couldn't see why I was asking it.

But I was quite clear that I would be able to do very little in terms of shaping and encouraging the life of the Church in the diocese unless the clergy wanted to work with me and were willing to trust me with some of their local information, priestly experience and personal skills. I needed them to tell me what they were good at doing, and what they thought needed to be done in their parish and deanery, and to give them encouragement and (as it turned out) permission. Some were eager to talk; others – naturally suspicious of enthusiastic and probably interfering bishops – were more reserved. Only one met me on the doorstep with the words, 'Hello. I'm N.M. and I've the freehold here. I plan to retire in 2011: do you want to come in?' Others had ritual initiation tests: one – at 9.30 in the morning – dismissed Sarah with the words, 'You'll find my wife in the church making coffee', before he turned to me and said, 'Would you like a drink?' and poured us both large tumblers of Irish whiskey. 'Another?' was the inevitable question that concluded the test, and thus fortified we wove our way down to the church to read Morning Prayer at breakneck speed, and so forged a splendid working understanding.

This voyage of discovery is equally true for any priest new to a parish – priests will want to know what lay people can give them for their ministry, and what the laity have learnt to do and discovered they are good at doing during the vacancy, and give them permission to go on doing it. It would be an enormous pity to weigh in and take it all back into clerical hands; what is needed is a straightforward assessment of what people are good at and enjoy doing, and what can properly be done only by a priest. Conversely, it is equally important for new priests to be asked what they are good at doing, and to be encouraged to do that too.

The geographical pattern

As the months of Lent went on and we moved around the diocese, I found my routes criss-crossing the landscape laterally rather than making a series of darts out of Salisbury and back in a kind of star-shaped, centripetal pattern. By building up a web of byways backwards and forwards across from one deanery to another, I began to get some sense of how the communications worked on the ground. Some links that look superficially obvious on a map turn out to have hidden geographical or social fault-lines on the ground; and a constant factor was how far off Salisbury often feels. I learnt where teenagers went to school and where people went to shop; I learnt where historic alliances and enmities still undermined relationships. In practical terms, this was enormously significant because it meant that I not only got to know the clergy and began to get a feel of what their ministry was like; I also came to know the social as well as physical geography of the diocese, and why one part felt so different from another.

The human resources

The result of that long extended Lenten period spent out and about was that I came back with a fairly clear picture of the human resources of the clergy of the diocese: where people were, some of the skills they had, how embedded they were in their way of doing things, and how ready they were to step out and either offer or ask for some kind of partnership. At the back of my mind initially was simply the building up of connections. I had an instinctive feel that the right way to start was to get some roots down, to get around and be there for a bit – a pattern that actually got me into the diocese as a listening presence in an incarnational way. I now believe with hindsight that this was a theologically appropriate way to start, but that was as a result of later reflection when I began to reflect more consciously on the nature of ministry. Originally it had just been a gut feeling that I should get out of the Close in Salisbury and travel round and get to know people.

Listening and dialogue

After Easter, I began to reflect on what I had learnt in order to try and articulate for the diocese as a whole the recurring threads of their concerns. We held a series of meetings in the summer and into the early autumn with the parish priests and churchwardens in each archdeaconry in order to play back what I had heard – what were the major themes which they thought needed to be explored.

I fed back to them three things:

- First, they were concerned with the Christian basics. How do we become more sure of our faith, and what patterns of education and formation will help?
- Second, many people were not confident about how to put their faith into practice. How do we learn to practise what we preach? How do we translate what we believe into action?
- Third, what are the deep roots in our spirituality? What sacrificial models of faith and worship lie beneath our attempts to lead the Christian life, and how should we reinforce them in our common life and worship?

Out of the feedback from these meetings I produced a series of questions for each parish, asking for the answers on a postcard. Given that this is what we have agreed are our principal concerns – formation, putting faith into practice and undergirding worship with a sacrificial sense of self-giving – what are you, in your parish, going to do about each of them?

This was the moment when things could have gone horribly wrong, when they were expecting to be told what to do, and to face yet another programme sent down from on high. In the face of seductive demands for 'firm leadership from the top', I was mercifully delivered from that classic mistake of telling people what to do, and instead said, 'These are the areas we have agreed are important. Let's support one another in taking a step forward in each of these areas, but you know best what needs doing in your church and in your locality so write me a postcard and let me know what you are going to do.'

Building relationships: a pattern of interdependence

This was partly saying to parish priests, 'I trust you.' This is crucial. Bishops have no option but to trust the parish clergy; they are the ones who actually know what is going on and know how to tailor any sense of mission for their context. And they in their turn have no option but to trust the people that they work with in their parishes. But we were also giving people permission to do the things that they naturally and instinctively felt were the right next steps for them. At the same time, we were helping to provide a framework in which people's concerns and the steps they were taking could be drawn together and given shape, so that they felt they were making a distinctive contribution to the wider life of the diocese as a whole as we supported one another.

This initial bit of work in the diocese was surprisingly successful in changing the style and feel of everybody's expectations of leadership. In other words, here was a conscious working out of the 'yours and mine' in the service that institutes and inducts a new parish priest. In that service the bishop reads out the legal document, and says as he hands it over: 'Receive this Cure of Souls which is both yours and mine, in the name of the Father, and of the Son and of the Holy Spirit.' This does not mean, 'Thank goodness you've agreed to come to this parish. Here it is; it's all yours. I've done my bit by getting you here, and apart from praying for you when it's your turn on the list, I hope I don't hear from you or of you for the next seven years at least.' Instead, it's an invitation to a partnership: to model a pattern of interdependence, rather than either a fawning dependence or a bloody-minded independence, neither of which is wholly unknown in the Church of England.

Where does ministry come from?

I was also hearing a lament, especially from lay people, about losing a sense of the local in terms of ministerial presence. Many parishes were in large teams or groups and felt geographically isolated from one another. The parish priest could live in only one of the villages up and down the valley, and however much he or she was present in others, that's not the same as actually living there. At a fairly early stage on my initial visits I had a particular encounter with a number of rural churchwardens. The new parish priest had not yet been instituted, so all the churchwardens had kindly turned out to meet me. It was the last day of partridge shooting in February so they were making a considerable sacrifice by stopping early that Saturday afternoon. As we stood around in a freezing church making polite conversation, one of them said, 'Bishop, when are we going to have our own parson?' to which I replied, 'Well, he's moving in next week and I'm coming to institute him in a fortnight's time, I think.' There was a bit of coughing and shuffling and it was clear that this answer would not quite do; so I tried again: 'Do you mean, when are you going to have a parson in your own parish?' Ah, that was more like it. So I said: 'Well, of course, you can have one almost as soon as you like.' His eyes lit up with surprise, and then clouded over as he wondered how much that was going to cost. So I made it explicit: 'You simply have to tell me which of *you* I should ordain.'

Rethinking vocation

In the end, the request for more clergy has meant turning the idea of vocation on its head. The local church needs to take a lead and not just wait until somebody appears fully fledged from a theological college with something miraculously acquired called 'a vocation'. The key question is, 'Who does the calling?' We need to say to the local church, 'It is your responsibility. Look carefully at the gifts that each person has, and then call one of them to lead your church life, to be a focus for pastoral care and to be the principal minister at worship.'

Until we actually turned it round like that, very few people thought of ministry as something other than sent, fully packaged. They expected ordained ministry to be dished out centrally, 'the bishop giving us someone to look after us'. These expectations were reinforcing that model of paternalistic pastoral care where parishes are the recipients and somebody else does all the sending and all the giving. But as we began to change that for a model of interdependence, then we began to discover that it is possible to move forward.

An Ordained Local Ministry Scheme develops

What local initiative in discerning gifts does is to unlock a lot of other interests, gifts and skills in its wake, and the pattern of training that we evolved in our pilot Ordained Local Ministry Scheme – drawing ordinands together with their tutor one week, and the next getting them to meet with their parish support groups to pass on what they learnt the previous week – has ensured a kind of pyramid learning that has been enormously beneficial, and is already producing a second wave of local ordinands. But more important than that, it has produced a core of parishioners who have grown confident in their faith, and have begun to think of what they can offer to the benefice, the deanery and even the diocese instead of being absorbed in what they can get for themselves in having their own priest.

The candidates who have emerged through this process have been splendid. People don't vote for candidates who rather fancy themselves in the role, and if they might be preaching to you for the next 30 years you are pretty careful who you put forward. Because they are rooted in their communities and trusted by them, I was at first ordaining them deacon relatively soon in their training – a key part of the role of a deacon is to be there and to listen – and they trained 'on the job'. But I did not ordain them priest until both they and the community that they served had shown signs of looking upwards and outwards, had begun to show a sense of responsibility for the Church as a whole.

Those diaconal skills – being there, attending to people and listening – were the very activities which I had found myself doing at the start of my ministry in Salisbury when I first arrived. But just because they are fundamental to the role of a deacon does not mean that priests or bishops or lay people should never do them. Quite the reverse. It is because they are so fundamental to all ministry that it is so important for the diaconate to highlight them. Being there, attending and listening are the essential first stages of engagement in any job or place, before any change can be contemplated. If change is simply imposed without a period of listening, the chances are that it will not have deep roots. On one level, this is basic common sense; but it is surprising how often experienced priests and bishops forget this basic stage, and their ministry fails to take root. True growth, true change will only happen if there has been patient engagement and good listening first.

New beginnings

We began this chapter by asking what it's like for everyone starting new enterprises; what do we do, what knowledge and skills do we try to acquire beforehand, how do we think about it, how do we map out the territory, how do we try and plan a move from A to B? So that is why I say at Inductions to clergy who are new to the diocese, 'Remember that you are a deacon as well as a priest, and operate like a deacon for a bit; go around and listen to what's going on, and try and attend to people's expressed needs. Discover what resources they have to offer to the ministry in this place, how they've taken responsibility for the things they think are important during the vacancy. Have some conversation with them about what they are good at, and let them show you where the signs of life are – what they think God is doing here. Tell them what you enjoy doing and what you're hopeless at, and refuse to let them hand back to you all the things they've discovered they can do. But you can't evaluate what you pick up unless you have actually got rooted in and engaged with the place and people, and the history of how things are as they are. So be a deacon first, and only then move into the distinctively priestly role.'

The pilgrimage pattern

The great thing about a pilgrimage is that you are on the way somewhere in the company of others. Knowing where you are and where you want to try and get to, and working out where the path lies so that you don't miss the turning, is what is important. One of the things that I think we are not very good at as clergy (and this applies to anyone who works with people) is helping people to be realistic about where they actually are. On one level everybody knows where they are; they are in Steeple Langford or Marlborough, Poole or Melbury Bubb or wherever. But knowing where they are in the sense of how they have got where they are, what their formation has led them to become – that kind of honest appraisal of one another as we start a new chapter of ministry – is quite hard and it takes somebody with skills to sit with you and work at it.

I know how useful it was for me to gain some insight about how I worked and therefore what I would need to do in terms of the crucial relationships with those who worked with me, and what I would need in terms of close colleagues to complement what I might bring. But starting a new phase of ministry isn't the only time when this is important. There are some key moments in people's lives when this whole map-making exercise – in the sense of knowing where people have come from in order to get here and then having a picture of where they want to get to – is really important. One such moment is when people are on the verge of retirement; another is for those in the sixth form who are starting to think about careers and therefore what university courses they might study; or those in mid-stream who begin to think about whether what they are studying will actually equip them to do what they want. They may be acquiring the wrong skills or have the wrong tools in their hands, and indeed as the map of the territory changes and the pathways become clearer, people may need to make major shifts. Sometimes we need the nerve to do that sooner rather than later. Because if you go three-quarters of the way there and then find that there is no bridge across the river, you have to trail all the way back, as people who journey without reading the map carefully discover to their cost. So reading the signs and consulting with your fellow travellers become more significant. That was certainly true on the pilgrimage to Compostela; listening to people who were finding things difficult, or who were walking back the other way and could tell us what lay ahead, were all quite important.

Glimpsing the pattern

When I had finished going round the diocese and consulting the churchwardens and clergy on what I thought I had heard, I was asked to reflect back to the whole diocese where we had got to in a Lent course which would communicate the style of this vision and help draw people into it.

I chose for that Lent course to do a series of studies on Luke 24, the story of the Journey to Emmaus. That extraordinarily vivid narrative has always fascinated me, but only as I began reflecting on it, commenting on it and thinking of how to draw people into it, did I realize for the first time how significant it is in terms of providing a model of the way the Church might live and work.

From that Lent course on Luke 24, from thinking through the Ordained Local Ministry Scheme (see page 8) and from the responses I got on the postcards from parishes all over the diocese, I began to sense an underlying shape to the way in which ministry and mission might develop. I began to detect that in Luke 24 there was not only a story of the early experience of the disciples as they came to faith and began to realize that the Lord was risen and present among them, especially in the breaking of the bread, but also a pattern that could reveal the way in which people today come to faith.

One of the catalysts for me in developing this thinking was a preliminary debate on Baptism at the General Synod. I had been speaking about recovering for the Church a pattern of staged development in the Initiation Rites, so that the natural stages of growth in faith could find some kind of echo in the liturgical cele-brations. Could we have less of a theology of instant conversion, please; that just wasn't everyone's experience. The next speaker was Gavin Reid, who had just run the Mission to London. To my surprise, his experience clearly echoed mine. The essence of what he said was that it takes on average about four years for people to come to faith, and while there may be a crucial moment you can point to with hindsight, it will be part of a process.

The Emmaus story and the shape of worship

So the Emmaus story and the pattern of formation for those coming to faith (which we began to develop in the Liturgical Commission as we were revising the Baptism and Confirmation rites for *Common Worship*) began to interact in my mind and I started to see a family likeness. At the same time, the Commission was learning about staged acts of worship – tuning the shape and sequence of the elements in an act of worship (or perhaps several over a period of months) to echo the natural stages in our experience. For new Christians, for example, for whom the sense of belonging is the first stage in feeling secure enough to explore the radical demands of the Christian faith, should we not provide a rite of welcome as a prelim-inary to their commitment to a pattern of learning before we ask whether they want to be baptized, rather than make full-blown baptism the first step? All that was running alongside our reflection on how the liturgy of the Church, whether it was a formal, sacra-mental celebration or a much less formal act of worship, actually acquired its shape and its structure. Where did its underlying power to catch people into the act and transform their lives come from? Again I began to see parallels between the basic structure of all litur-gical worship and the Emmaus story more generally.

As I reflected on that, I started to see that this same model was also reflected in the way in which people understood their place in the Church even when they weren't thinking of the baptismal journey, but merely thinking about their membership and their responsibili-ties as members of the baptized to engage in the Church's work, to share the gospel and to live out their faith in their pattern of rela-tionships and the activities in which they were engaged.

Out of these strands there began to form at the back of my mind a coherent pattern, which this book explores.

Searching for coherence

One of the things that is very difficult when you step into any new ministerial task – and I think it is even more true for lay people than for clergy – is to say how is there to be coherence between who I am, what I believe and how I try to live. It is a search that all Christian people are engaged in, though it is perhaps particularly sharply focused for those with authorized ministerial responsibility.

These essentially autobiographical reflections have been trying to give you some sense of what has been happening to me over these years since I came to Salisbury. The move into episcopal ministry here has been the catalyst, but there are many ingredients: the clergy and people in the parishes of the diocese; my colleagues on the Liturgical Commission, and the way that liturgical revision has challenged us to do worship better and make it engage with how to be Church; the need to provide a Lent course for the diocese; working at a theology of ministry both for the Ordained Local Ministry Scheme for the diocese and in preparation for the revision of the ordinal; trying to deliver a coherent and compact theology of ministry and mission for our episcopal brothers in the Church in the Province of Sudan. All these are contributory threads.

What happens in the pages that follow is the working out of an over-arching matrix or pattern for the Christian life which is God-given and which provides unity and coherence between a number of the different activities of church-making in which we are all engaged. This working out begins with an analysis of its biblical source, which is the subject of the next chapter. From this is developed a basic pattern which I hope is simple enough for anyone with the elements of the Christian faith in their bones to grasp and articulate. This basic pattern serves as a map to show the connections between the Christian faith, the Christian life and Christian worship, and suggests how our corporate journey of faith and personal integrity as seekers can be drawn together into a coherent whole.

2 | The Emmaus Story Unfolds God's Pattern

The fourfold pattern: attending, engaging, transforming and energizing for mission

Luke is the most vivid storyteller of the four evangelists, and his narratives have an extraordinary power to grip the imagination. The other Gospels have nothing like the annunciation or the birth narratives, no equivalent of the Good Samaritan or the Prodigal Son, and above all, no resurrection narrative to match the Journey to Emmaus.

The Emmaus story

Like all powerful narratives, the Journey to Emmaus is a story that unfolds in stages. It begins with the leaden footsteps of the disciples, trailing back to where they lived after the bottom had fallen out of their world. The charismatic leader on whom they had built their hopes of a transformed world had been executed; they had seen it with their own eyes. That was the end.

So they are amazed that the stranger who falls in with them on the road appears not to know about what has happened in Jerusalem over this last week; how the authorities had combined to get rid of the prophetic young leader who had attracted quite a following. It was true that his attack on their religious institutions had challenged the stability of the 'arrangement' between their leaders and the occupying power. It looked as if this Passovertime might have brought another release, this time from the domination of the hated Romans. And the stranger hadn't heard a thing?

It takes them a few miles to tell the story, and then an extraordinary thing happens: their companion begins a highly detailed scripture lesson. He takes them right back into the narratives they know so well. Of course there would be a moment when the God of their fathers would raise up a Messiah to lead his people out of slavery and into the long-promised freedom in the land that was theirs. But have they read the texts carefully? What kind of a person would he be? Was he to be a successful soldier, or do the scriptures suggest a rather more complex picture of a leader, chosen by God, who might have to take the failings of his people on his own shoulders?

He goes on so long that he is still expounding the texts when they reach the village. Night is falling, and it seems inhospitable not to invite him in. Anyway, the fascinating exposition makes them have second thoughts about what had happened in Jerusalem. Was the demonstration they were caught up in the prelude to a political revolution as they had supposed, or was there a deeper, more spiritual purpose in Jesus' challenge to the authorities that they had missed? So they ask him to stay. Then, as the meal begins, they invite their remarkable guest to say the blessing. He takes the bread, blesses it and breaks it, and in a flash they tumble to who it is.

Suddenly all the pieces of the jigsaw fall into place, and they know that the person who had walked the way with them is the same Jesus who had broken the bread like that at the Last Supper. He had told them to go on doing that to recapture that sense of intimacy, but when they saw his body broken on the cross they had known it was all over. But it wasn't. He had walked with them, and they must tell the others at once.

So they rise, and without a thought for their empty stomachs or aching feet, set out back to Jerusalem to find the disciples and tell them what they have experienced. How they had walked with Jesus, but failed to recognize him as they were so preoccupied with their own sense of loss. How he had taught them the true meaning of his mission, and how he had reinforced his promise to be present in the breaking of the bread.

The fourfold structure of the narrative

This vivid narrative story of the Journey to Emmaus (Luke 24.13–35) provides a model for how God attends to us, shares our life, changes it and then energizes us to continue his work. The account is divided into four parts, and this fourfold division provides a fundamental structure for Christian worship, ministry and witness.

In the first section (verses 13–24), Jesus draws out the disciples' story. At the start of the journey, the stranger falls in with the despondent disciples, and gets them to tell him what they think has happened. This centres on what they had hoped for and their sense of the failure of Jesus' mission, which had ended with his death.

In the second section (verses 25–27) Jesus sets the story of God's doings alongside theirs. After listening to their interpretation of their experience, Jesus tells them that the scriptures (our Old Testament) hold the key to understanding the events they describe, explaining that the kind of Messiah that would fulfil God's purposes would be one who suffered and died for his people. The disciples still fail to recognize the teacher who journeys with them.

In the third section (verses 28–31) the disciples' eyes are opened and they are transformed by the experience. At the supper-table, their guest takes, blesses and breaks the bread, and gives it to them. This is a moment of transformation, as they recognize in their guest the one who had done this at that Last Supper. It was Jesus, who had promised to be present with them whenever they repeated those actions.

In the fourth section (verses 32–35) the disciples are energized to take action. This experience of the living Christ in their midst fires them. They forget themselves and their exhaustion in their concern to tell the other disciples, and return straightaway to Jerusalem to share with them 'what had happened to them on the way'.

The pattern of God's dealing with his people

The whole Emmaus episode, with its fourfold pattern of attending, engaging, transforming and energizing, is a model of how God deals with his people throughout their history.

1 Us and our self-centred story

The Old Testament, especially Genesis 2—5, recalls the breakdown of our relationship with God, spelt out in the collapse of harmony and trust between human beings and the natural world and between one person and another. In spite of our repeated unfaithfulness, our failure to keep the Covenant, God remains faithful to his promise. This is the theme of Hosea. But in spite of God's continuing loving kindness, we take no notice: we want our desires, our needs, our wills to triumph. That is the human story of sin.

2 God comes to share our life

After repeated messages through the events of his chosen people's history (summarized in Jesus' exposition in Luke 24.25–27 as the

Law and the Prophets) which are either ignored or at best only believed half-heartedly, God in the end decides to speak with his people face to face (Hebrews 1.1–2). In the incarnation God sets aside his majesty and power, shares our life, and is born as a weak and vulnerable baby (Philippians 2.5–11). This is so that we might have 'the knowledge of the glory of God in the face of Jesus Christ' (2 Corinthians 4.6, AV).

3 The God who shares our human nature then changes our life
By his dying and rising, Jesus shows that death does not destroy his relationship either with us or with his Father. His resurrection re-unites us with the Father, restores our relationships with one another and the created order, makes us whole, and establishes the New Creation.

4 Then God entrusts us with continuing his work
By his Holy Spirit, God gives his people not only gifts but the ability to share them so that his work can be continued and extended. Christ's body, the Church, has all these gifts. When turned in on itself it can be Babel – a disabling chaos of competition; but when turned outward, the power and energy can be a means of uniting everyone – a true Pentecost (1 Corinthians 12).

At the heart of this pattern are the two things that God has done for us in Christ: first, he shares our life; then he changes it. But this twofold 'Christ-event' does not stand in isolation: it has a long prologue and a continuing epilogue. In the long prologue of humanity's search for meaning that precedes the Christ-event, the on–off relationship with God is characterized by long periods of turning away from him interspersed with only brief flashes of insight, in spite of a deep longing to be known and loved. The biblical record speaks of human sin and broken covenant relation-ships while God, like a patient husband, longs for his unfaithful people's return. The epilogue charts the history of the Church from the moment of Pentecost, when God hands over the responsibility to continue what had been initiated in Christ – a continuing pattern of engagement and transformation.

After millennia of seeking contact with humanity, and hoping that they will return to him, what God does is to run out to meet us, like the father in Luke 15.20. First, in Christ he shares our life; then he changes it; and finally, by his Spirit, equips us to continue this core pattern of engagement and transformation that is the Church's continuing task to bring his kingdom into being.

This development into a fourfold pattern of how God works among us is reflected in:

- the pattern of our worship;
- the pattern of our ministry;
- the pattern of our mission.

Each of these areas of our common life and witness shows the same theological movement, from God's engagement with our human condition to the change he brings and the responsibility he shares with us in continuing that pattern. Here in summary is the pattern that is worked out more fully in the rest of this book.

The pattern of our worship

1 The Gathering or Preparation
The advent or time of expectation in our worship, when we long for God's coming and tune our ears and eyes to recognize his presence
As we come to worship, we bring ourselves, our concerns, our joys and our sorrows. As the community gathers, these individual and personal concerns need drawing together to be shaped, challenged, offered and transformed. The Preparation at the Eucharist begins with a Greeting and welcome. There is opportunity in the acts of penitence and hymns of praise to express our sorrow and regret and our joys and thanksgiving, and for these individual threads to be woven into a corporate picture of the community as they are gathered together and offered to God in the prayer of the Collect.

2 The Liturgy of the Word
The Christmas, or celebration of the Word made flesh, coming among us to engage with us
In the readings from the Old Testament and St Paul we rehearse the encounter with God's story as handed down in the Prophets and the (new) Law. We read the balanced diet that the Lectionary sets before us; we do not choose the bits *we* want to hear, or that support *our* views. The readings challenge us over a complete year by setting the

whole of God's story alongside the story of our own world. Then as Advent leads to Christmas, so we greet the living Word, Jesus himself, in the Gospel. That is why the book for the Gospel reading is a specially bound one or the best and largest Bible that can be found, and why it is carried into the middle of the assembly for the Gospel to be read 'among' the people, not 'at' them ('. . . but I am among you as one who serves' (Luke 22.27, NIV)). This is God speaking to us face to face in Jesus: 'The Word was made flesh, and pitched his tent among us. And we beheld his glory, the glory as of the only begotten of the Father, full of grace and truth' (John 1.14). '. . . Jesus stood among them' (John 20.19; Luke 24.36). 'Among' is the key word. The way Jesus engages with his disciples then and now is different from the more distant way God is represented as speaking to his people in the Old Testament.

The purpose of the sermon is to interweave or zip together the story of what God has done for us in Christ and the story of what and who we are, so that the two lock together and one interprets the other. The sermon should help us understand how God has taken us into his story and made us a part of his life with a job for us to do. Sermons play a vital part in relating our story to the story of what God has done and helping people to see the connections.

The sermon leads naturally into prayer for those whose needs we bring with us so that they too may be woven into God's story.

3 The Liturgy of the Sacrament
God's transforming of our life by taking it into the passion and resurrection of Jesus Christ's dying and rising
In the celebration of the Sacrament, God changes us. The pattern of what happened at the supper-table in Emmaus repeats the four actions of the Last Supper. The living presence of Christ is discovered in our midst, when we do this in obedience to his command. The Church has recognized those four actions and set them at the heart of our worship.

1 We take bread and wine and prepare them on the table. In that bread and wine we lay ourselves before God to be blessed, broken and used in his service.
2 In the Eucharistic Prayer we give thanks to the Father through the Son in the power of the Spirit: praising the Father for his creation and his faithfulness in spite of our turning away; welcoming his

coming to share our life in Christ, and, after the narrative of the Last Supper, recalling his death and resurrection, the transforming events of his life; praying for the coming of his Spirit to make the gifts holy, so that we who share them may be transformed too, and our broken lives made whole.

3 The bread is broken as a sign of Christ's death. As Jesus' death on the cross is what released his life for all to share, so the broken bread enables us all to share in his life, and so be made one (cf. John 12.24).

4 We receive the body and blood of Christ, and so are transformed from being broken individuals, isolated from each other and God by sin, into being members together in the risen Christ. We are one body, united with the whole Church everywhere and throughout the ages (cf. 1 Corinthians 10.17).

4 The Dismissal
The moment of Pentecost, when the scattered disciples finally realized that God had given them all they needed to engage in their apostolic mission

In the final prayer we pray, 'Send us out in the power of your Spirit to live and work to your praise and glory.' The end of worship involves us in a commitment, strengthened by God's blessing, to go and put into practice what we have become – a new community, fired by God's Spirit to do his will and help his kingdom come. We are to be doers of the Word, and not hearers only (James 1.22), or we shall be accused of not practising what we preach. The final prayers and Dismissal are most visibly a 'little Pentecost' in the Baptism or Confirmation rites, when the newly baptized and confirmed are each given a lighted candle, with the charge 'Shine as a light in the world, to the glory of God the Father' (cf. Matthew 5.16).

The pattern of our ministry

Christ hands over to his Church the responsibility of continuing his ministry. Every baptized person who has tumbled to it that this is what they are is called to use their gifts to minister in his name. But while each of us has a ministry to exercise, not all of us are called to be ministers, ordained to hold before the Church a specific focus of Christ's ministry – his sharing our life, his redemptive transformation of it and his handing over to us the responsibility of continuing this pattern of engagement and transformation.

Within the ministry of all the baptized, this threefold pattern of God's activity in response to our human story is given visible expression in the historic threefold ministry of the Church. To the broken, self-absorbed world of human striving, God in Christ comes among us, raises us up and equips us to live his life. This saving activity of incarnation, redemption and sanctification is focused in the life of the Church by the three historic orders of ministry. It is these orders that give a Christ-like shape to the Church, and remind the whole Church (not just the ordained) that we are his body, and that we minister in his name and by his strength and authority alone.

1 The ministry of a deacon

The incarnation is the foundation of God's redeeming activity. It comes first. 'That which God did not assume, he did not redeem,' says Gregory Nazianzus, making it clear that for God to change people, he needed to engage with us and share human life first. In the same way, the ministry of the deacon is the foundation of all ordained ministry. You are a deacon first, and even if later you become a priest or a bishop, you never cease to be a deacon. The incarnation is about God coming among us to share our life, and setting aside the trappings of pomp and power (Philippians 2.5–11). The deacon focuses this sense of God sharing our life and engaging with us directly by making God's incarnation, his becoming rooted in human life, central in the Church. Priests and bishops who forget that they are deacons too often try to use their position to get their own way, forgetting that Jesus taught us differently – that authority and kingship are rooted in service, not in the capricious use of power ('It shall not be so among you . . .' (Matthew 20.26, RSV)). This is the heart of what ministry means, though government ministers and even prime ministers do not always seem to act as if they know this! Perhaps this is because we have lost the sense of the ordained as signposts to the whole of the *laos* or people of God of whom they are a part. So often we have colluded with a theology of ministry that says the ordained are there to minister *instead of* the whole people rather than saying that the ordained are to be *a focus*, a constant reminder, of what every Christian is called to be, which is why the ordained carry the Church's authority to minister in a representative way.

In coming among us to share our life and engage with us face to face, God in Christ draws his disciples into a ministry of love and service by washing his disciples' feet, commanding them to go and do likewise. In John 13, Jesus teaches by example. When that Gospel is read at the Ordination of Deacons, and even more when the bishop washes the newly ordained deacons' feet, we are reminded of just how fundamental this ministry is, and how often we are tempted to try to bring a change to people without that necessary engagement first. The deacon's ministry is about this kind of engagement with the particularities of human life. That is why a deacon is appointed to serve in a particular place, to take root in a community, just as Christ was born in a particular place – Bethlehem – at a particular time – 2,000 years ago.

> **The liturgical ministry of the deacon**
> It is also why in worship it has traditionally been the deacon who has brought the Book of the Gospels into the assembly and been charged with reading the Gospel among the people; with gathering up the particularities which give substance to the prayers of intercession; with preparing the table and distributing the Holy Communion; with translating this sense of renewed commitment into practical tasks of being the Church in the coming week, and with sending out the assembled church to do them. This sense of being God's agent, the go-between who engages with the task, means that deacons are active in the community. That is why deacons wear their stoles tied round their albs: so that they are ready for action.

2 The ministry of the priest

If the focus of a deacon's ministry is the incarnation, the focus of a priest's is our redemption. If a deacon shows to the Church how God in Christ shares our life, the priest reveals how God in Christ changes it. That is why the priest is the minister who presides over the sacraments, those rites in the Church where we celebrate the change that God in Christ brings about. Whether we are talking of baptism or the Eucharist, individual change or corporate renewal, the same is true. The priest's task is to reconcile, to draw people and communities together; to bless people in God's name; to preach and teach so that people's lives are changed; and to intercede like that great High Priest 'who ever lives to make intercession for us' (Hebrews 7.25).

At the heart of the priest's life is the one, perfect self-offering of Christ to the Father. This sacrificial action has what St Paul describes as 'the upward call of God in Christ Jesus' (Philippians 3.14, RSV) as its theme, and transformation as its key. The power to change is not one of manipulation to get what we want; it is the surrender of our wills to God's, that his kingdom come, his will be done. This is the mystery of the cross, which looks like a failure to the unbeliever, but turns out to be the power of God, perfected in our human weakness. The resurrection turns the cross upside down: the tree of death becomes the tree of life; where life was lost, there life has been restored. This reversal, this turning of the world's expectations upside down, is the heart of the mystery of the Eucharist, where the priest takes the one bread he has just consecrated to be the body of Christ, and breaks it into pieces, that we, the broken members of Christ's body, all may receive a fragment of that broken bread and so be restored to life and union with God.

The priestly life, then, has as its focus a sense of being drawn into the sacrificial self-offering of Christ to the Father; it is a life of constant tension and continuous change, and the challenge is to hold this pattern of continuing change before the whole Church as a never-ending challenge to our being satisfied with where we've got to.

3 The ministry of a bishop

The bishop is still both priest and deacon. The bishop is rooted in the particularity of the diocese, which is why a bishop must live there among the people, not, as in earlier centuries, in London at Court. The bishop is there to engage with them, to listen to them and to serve them; this is made visible when the bishop washes the feet of the newly ordained deacons at an ordination. Still a priest, the bishop continues the ministry of reconciliation, drawing people by word and example into the body of Christ, the wounded healer, that we may be drawn into his perfect self-offering to the Father.

The bishop's most distinctive ministry is to hand on the apostolic witness to the risen Christ: 'I delivered to you what I also received, that Christ Jesus was raised . . .' (1 Corinthians 15.3). But you can only hand on a tradition if there is a continuing community into which people are being woven all the time. So the focus of the bishop's ministry is building the community of faith, so that the tradition may be handed on. This is most visible when baptizing and confirming new Christians and ordaining deacons and priests. Confirmations and Ordinations also mark the moment where the Church in all its diversity can be recognized to be essentially one with the Spirit-filled tradition of the early apostles. The day of Pentecost (Acts 2) reverses the consequences of the Tower of Babel (Genesis 11): the same phenomenon – a rich diversity of tongues – is seen not as a sign of chaos or fragmentation, but – to a Church looking outwards – as a sign of engagement with all God's people everywhere. As well as providing a focus for unity, the bishop's responsibility is to turn people to face outwards, in mission. A bishop's crook or pastoral staff has two ends: a hook to draw people together in one fold, and a sharp end to prod them into action, leaving the security of the holy huddle.

A bishop does not do this because he possesses some power of his own. He exercises his ministry to order and shape the Church, thus making visible the commission given by Christ to his apostles to draw everyone into one fold, and to baptize all nations. A bishop is the sign of the continuing activity of the Spirit in the Church to draw people into unity and to energize them for mission.

The Church's mission

The Emmaus pattern of attending, engaging, transforming and energizing forms the basis of our strategy for mission as well. Whether we see the Church's mission in terms of ministry to individuals or to whole communities, the same stages apply.

1 The prerequisite for mission is *attending*. Unless we first attend to what is going on and what is being said, and who is saying or doing what, we will not train ourselves to listen first, before we do or say anything. Finding out from other people's accounts of what is going on, where the signs of life are, is vital if true engagement is to follow. This is true of a new minister arriving to serve a community. It is equally true of ministry to an individual. If we think that we have the answers before we listen to what we are being told, the chances are that we will spend our energies in answering the questions that no one is actually asking.
2 After attending, *engaging*. The Anglican tradition has prided itself on engaging. Historically, our churches are set in the heart of our towns and villages, and are often the most significant buildings

there. Our sense of place means that we think it important that the clergy, who are the visible sacramental focus of the Church's ministry, should live in the communities where they minister. By tradition, the Anglican parish priest is a person who ministers to and prays for everyone who lives in the parish, churchgoers or not. This rural idyll, exemplified in our folk memory by priests like George Herbert and Francis Kilvert, the diarist, has its counterpart in the urban ministry that developed in the wake of the Industrial Revolution. Clergy came to live in the heart of the new developments as new parishes were created out of the historic city-centre parish. The heroes of these days are priests like Fr Dolling in the dockyard slums of Portsmouth or Fr Jameson who planned the Leeds housing programme in the 1930s. There too parish priests are ministers of Word and Sacrament for the whole community, as their book-lined studies – studies, not offices – and hospitable tables should make clear. They are as much at home in clubs and pubs as in church. They are known figures in the community, with as ready access to people and institutions as people have to them; and the nature of their pastoral ministry is revealed as much in how they live as in what they say. They are a voice for the voiceless and free from the constraints of being in anyone's pocket, socially or politically, which is why the parson (the 'person') is a figure of continuing interest and importance.

And this is not just true of a long-established pattern of incarnational presence in England. The same is true – or should be – wherever the Church tries to follow the example of Christ. Salisbury is blessed with a remarkable overseas link with the Province of the Sudan, from which we gain more than we could ever give. In the southern part of that vast country, community as well as infrastructure has been destroyed by nearly forty years of civil war. A young priest, Francis Loyo, found himself consecrated bishop for the Diocese of Rokon, near the front line of the fighting. So he set out to go there and minister to his people. When Bishop Francis arrives in Rokon to find the few people who have not fled because of the fighting, what does he do? He does not send for help. He himself works with whoever is there to build schools and a church, an orphanage and a pharmacy, establish farms and a water supply, and by living among those who are traumatized by the war he rebuilds their confidence in human community. The second step in mission therefore is to engage with people and work alongside them. 'Preach the gospel', said St Francis to Brother Lawrence. 'Use words if you must.'

3 Engaging creates the conditions for *transformation*. It is this working together – not the leaders telling others what to do – that creates the conditions in which the spark of God's transforming energy may fly across the gap between people or communities. This transformation is not something that we make happen: it is God's doing. Our task is to create the conditions in which God's amazing grace can get to work (1 Corinthians 3.6). Too much energy is often expended on trying to manipulate the outcome in the way that we want it to happen, when the heart of our mission should be prayer – Jesus' prayer to the Father, 'not my will, but thine, be done'. If we substitute our activity for prayer, then we may not have the energy or attention to hear or see what it is that God is trying to do with or through us to bring his will about or make his kingdom come. At the heart of this transforming possibility is a sense of partnership.

4 It is partnership that is *energizing*. It is this spark that jumps across the gap, this sense of being fused together in a collaborative pattern of work, which gives people of both communities the sense that they are being taken further than either could get on their own. That is where the energy to put vision into practice is generated, and only this kind of energy will make things happen. This is where the Word becomes active, 'sharper than any two-edged sword', and we see the vision of a transformed order taking root in how people live their lives and choose their priorities. It is this kind of transformation that changes not just individuals, but societies.

As an example of how this kind of transformation and energizing happens, I recall the experience of the provost of a cathedral in East Germany in the years immediately before and after the Berlin Wall came down. He explained to me that his cathedral had played a significant part in the weeks leading up to the collapse of East Germany by staying open until late at night and providing a safe space for people to meet and share their dreams. The cathedral seemed to be coming into its own as a safe space for young people especially, and they had great hopes that when the old order crumbled people might turn again to the Christian faith. So they were entirely thrown off balance when it became apparent that they had served their purpose. In the new world, the safe space was no longer needed by the liberated young. A new confidence had emerged, and the cathedral had to come to terms with the painful fact that they had had their moment. There was not going to be a great flooding back to church; the hospitality they had provided had been the catalyst in building a new sense of trust and common purpose. That was a proper contribution of the churches, but they had served their purpose in transformation of the human community.

3 | The Shape of Worship Embraces Us

The Eucharist

In the Eucharist there are two twin peaks when the two core things that God has done in Christ for his people – sharing our life and then transforming it – are made visible. These are the two moments in the liturgy which bring into focus what God has done for us in sharing our life in his incarnate Word and the transforming of that life by his act of sacrificial love on the cross. The first of these high points in the liturgy is the proclamation of the Gospel, and the second is the Breaking of the Bread.

But these high points do not stand alone. They have a prologue and an epilogue in the whole fourfold drama of the eucharistic action of which they are the peaks.

By the time Luke's Gospel was being formed, the essential fourfold shape of the Eucharist, gathered around these two peaks that reflect God sharing and then changing our life, was becoming clear. While those who describe the eucharistic liturgy are sometimes tempted to think in twofold terms of a Liturgy of the Word followed by a Liturgy of the Sacrament, this twofold structure needs a context – a gathering and a sending out – if the liturgy is both to engage with the worshippers and to inspire them to action.

As Chapter 2 makes clear, the Emmaus story in Luke 24.13–35 has four stages. They mark a process of the two disciples' slow re-formation. In spite of Jesus' teaching throughout his ministry, the disciples had been devastated by the apparent failure of his entire mission, and had to be slowly taught yet again that it is death that leads to life. The Eucharist, like the Emmaus narrative, has that re-formatting character. It both rehearses the Christian story and engages us in it.

Consider the Emmaus narrative in more detail. First, the two disciples, who are trailing back home mulling over their disappointment, are joined by a stranger who asks them what they are talking about. Prompted by this question, they need little further encouragement to confess their dashed expectations, and pour out the whole story of what has happened. Second, the stranger now takes the lead, tells them that they are fools not to have made the connections, and gives them a prolonged biblical exposition so that they can work it out for themselves. But the penny still does not drop. Third, the two disciples reach home and press the stranger, who has clearly been planning to go further, to stay. He comes in, sits at table with them, and then takes, blesses and breaks the bread. And suddenly, says St Luke, 'their eyes were opened, and they recognised him, and he vanished from their sight'. Fourth, fired with excitement at the biblical exposition and the breaking of the bread, which has suddenly made sense of the real presence of the living Lord to them, they leap up from the table and set out back for Jerusalem at once to tell the others, the despondent, weary journey of the afternoon forgotten.

In this story Luke – how consciously we cannot know – models the pattern of engagement and transformation at the heart of the eucharistic action by which the Church nourishes her life on Christ. And although you can make a simple twofold shape for the Eucharist, of Word (our engagement with Christ in the Liturgy of the Word) and Sacrament (our transformation in the Liturgy of the Sacrament), that scarcely does justice to the subtlety of Luke's emerging theology in this story; a story which weaves the remembering of the Last Supper, the real presence of Christ at Emmaus and the pilgrimage pattern of energized discipleship together under the overarching pattern of the Christ who shares our life, and then changes it.

To recapitulate the four stages of Luke's narrative and set them alongside the shape of the Eucharist, we have this fourfold shape which corresponds closely to the sections in the Gospel.

1 *The Gathering*, during which the assembly, who bring with them the story of their lives in their community during the week, is constituted by singing together, recalled in penitence to its baptismal status, and prepared to receive the Word of God. This section is summed or collected up in the Collect.

2 *The Liturgy of the Word*, during which the assembly engages with the Word, as the story of what God has done in Christ is set alongside the community's experience, and in the sermon the implications are teased out for prayer and action.

3 *The Liturgy of the Sacrament*, during which the assembly is offered
  the possibility of transformation as they are incorporated into the
  one, perfect self-offering of Christ to the Father and receive the
  body and blood of Christ by faith with thanksgiving.
4 *The Dismissal*, when the assembly is reminded to put into practice
  the new life they have received, and are sent out into the community to do it.

The Gathering

First, the assembly gathers, conscious of being on the way and eager
to tell its story – the story of what has happened since we last met.
That will include thanksgivings and praise for what has happened as
well as some penitential honesty about our failings. This penitence
is part of reviewing what has happened, though it ought not to
dominate in the way it often seems to: there is a strand in the
Anglican tradition which says that a service without an act of penitence is hardly worth the name. But looking on the past in a positive
way is also important, and people have done good as well as bad,
which is why the penitential element should be kept firmly in proportion. In the disciples' conversation as they walk to Emmaus, we
see them not so much penitent as disappointed, trying to make
sense of their failed expectations. So for us too, perhaps what is
more important is the tuning in, the learning again to attend to God
and to each other, to listen to the song of the angels to which the
Gloria makes reference, and to keep an expectant silence, pushing
our expectations to the limit.

   At the Eucharist I attended in an abbey in Brittany, the Community gathered with their guests in a kind of narthex or gathering
space in front of the doors to the abbey church itself. There was an
informal welcome by the Prior, and guests and visitors were asked to
introduce themselves briefly. We were invited to say why we had
come – what we were expecting spiritually of our visit – and then
the Prior said a word about the Community's vision of where it was
going and linked that to some words from the Epistle. He then led
us in some singing together, during which the presiding celebrant
and others entered, led by the deacon with the Book of the Gospels.
After the penitential rite – a reflective and extended Kyrie eleison –
we entered the abbey church singing the Gloria, and when we had
found our places, the opening rite was concluded with the Collect.
Later, after the altar had been prepared with the gifts, a second

movement occurred, and we were all included in one great ellipse in the spacious open sanctuary, standing round the altar for the whole of the liturgy of the sacrament. After the post-Communion prayer, we all went back singing to the narthex for the blessing and dismissal.

That would be a novel experience to those used to an English parish church, where as a visitor you are often given a bewildering clutch of books and leaflets and shown to a pew (though these days the verger rarely shuts the pew door behind you!). All the same, it is rather like being shown to a seat in the cinema; once you're there, it's yours and you stick to it. The way people are greeted, allowed to find their own space and yet are given a sense of being welcomed into a community that is on the move is not easy to achieve in our over-furnished churches. As the community of regular worshippers, we sometimes forget, like the disciples on the way to Emmaus, to ask about, or even notice, the strangers in our midst. In the middle of all the clutter of managing different books, finding a place, listening to interminable notices and getting up and down as choirs, clergy and whoever process in, we need to remember that the Greeting, silent prayer and a Collect are the bare bones of gathering the community for worship: everything else is padding.

The Liturgy of the Word

Second, we set the story of who we are, where we are coming from and where we hope to go alongside the story of what God has done for his people. Our ears may be full of the sound of our own voices, and we may think we know the parts of God's story that we would like to hear, and that speak to where we are. But the purpose of a Lectionary, a set of readings chosen by the Church and read every-where on that day, is to make sure that we are not only fed a balanced diet of biblical readings, but are also confronted with a number of passages we might not choose to hear, because they may challenge our comfortable assumptions. At the heart of this part of the Eucharist, as on the walk to Emmaus, are the words of Jesus himself. In the proclamation of the Gospel we are offered a direct encounter with the living Word; that is why we rise and may accom-pany the Gospel with lights and incense, as we expect to meet our Lord and Saviour in person. And it is also why small rituals like taking the Gospel Book round the assembly to be reverenced after the Gospel has been read are important. In that way each person is offered a direct encounter with the incarnate Son, the living Word, as the worshippers in a Jewish community are offered the chance of touching the scrolls with the fringes of their prayer shawls as they are carried past on their way back to the tabernacle.

It is the preacher's task to make this encounter with Jesus a living one, where the incarnate Word is enabled to take root, and the radical change in us that the Gospel demands can be helped on its way. It is this interaction between Christ and his people and all that we bring with us that should shape the Prayers of the People, where the skilful task of sifting, discernment and concise expression is traditionally entrusted to that liturgical go-between, the deacon.

The Liturgy of the Sacrament

Third, although those disciples were weary, and the penny had not yet dropped, they still invited the stranger to step over the threshold with the traditional blessing 'Peace be with you' as he came in. The liturgy, like the work of our redemption, does not end with engagement, with the encounter with the living Word. Actual change, not just the chance to think about it intellectually, is what our salvation offers. So does the eucharistic liturgy.

So after the Greeting of Peace comes the preparation of the gifts upon the table, in which we see – in St Augustine's words – 'the mystery of ourselves' upon the altar. In the great Thanksgiving we bless God for his creation and our redemption in Christ's self-offering, praying that by the power of his Holy Spirit we may feed on him and so be made one with God in this foretaste of the heavenly banquet. Then in the most powerful sign in this part of the Eucharist, the bread which has just been consecrated to be the body of Christ is broken. There before our eyes, as it was for the disciples at Emmaus, is the sign of the death, of the body broken on the cross. It is in the moment of the breaking of the bread that their eyes were opened, and the fragments of their memory and experience were tumbled together to produce a life-changing transformation, as they realized that Christ was really present.

As we receive the broken fragment of the consecrated bread into our hands, we too are offered transformation: a change from being the broken, discordant and fragmentary people that we are into being renewed and whole, members of one single body, ready to act as one. We have been caught up into the one perfect sacrifice of Christ to the Father, and that reshapes the direction of our lives. We no longer live for ourselves but for him who died and was raised for our salvation. If the moment of the breaking of the bread offers us an experience of Good Friday, then receiving the sacrament brings a moment of Easter, of being known and valued as ourselves like Mary Magdalene.

The Dismissal

No wonder then that, fourth, we are impatient to be up and doing. 'Did not our hearts burn within us on the way, while he opened the scriptures to us?' said the disciples. And they were off and away without a second thought. It is tempting to think of the Eucharist as if it were an end in itself, a wonderful pre-echo of a privileged heaven. But there is a rubric at the end, *The ministers and people depart*, and it is there for the same reason that the last section of the Eucharist is called the Dismissal, and the whole action is sometimes called the Mass. The root of these words is *missa*, the past participle of the Latin verb which means 'sent', from which our word 'mission' comes. The Church, changed by the celebration of the Eucharist, has been reshaped out of a lot of broken and fragmentary individuals into a united body, ready for action. We are sent out as apostles to live out what we have become, people transformed by the sacrificial love of God in Christ. Here is our moment of Pentecost, of taking responsibility for being what we have become – Christ's body on earth now.

The Eucharist offers us the shape for life, for the mission and engagement of the Church. This pattern of engagement and transformation is not something once delivered to the saints and played out daily or weekly in the liturgy as a reminder of a golden, but irretrievably past, age. It is the pattern for our growth in Christ now and always. This means that our participating in it is not only for our personal salvation, but also for mission, for our engagement with God's world for its salvation, its reshaping and renewal. We have God's people to care for and engage with directly: a Gift-Aid cheque in an envelope is not the same as personal engagement. We have governments with selfish interests, wanting to appeal to the voters' pockets to stay in power; so we have petrol priced to burn holes in the ozone layer on the one hand while we spend millions on cancer research with the other. We have fear and suspicion, those enemies of peace, stalking the land instead of truth and righteousness because what people are most afraid of is a real meeting with each other that is bound to change us. The offering of our lives that we make in worship cannot be satisfied with doing nothing; it calls us to a programme for action to make our world a better place. In other words, to celebrate the Eucharist together and do nothing about feeding the hungry is an act of blasphemy.

That has been the shape of the eucharistic celebration from the days of the apostles to now, and I recount it in order to make the pattern clear, and to suggest some ways in which parishes might make this eucharistic theology visible in the way in which we order our lives as Church.

The classic ingredients of worship

In the offering of worship to God, there are several major ingredients, running on a number of different levels.

1 Structure and shape

First, there is the structure or shape revealed by the historic practice and developing tradition of the Church. The evolution of this pattern that I have been teasing out can be traced from the early days of the Church. It is grounded in the experience recorded in the New Testament of those disciples who had been there at the Last Supper, witnessed the crucifixion and then had met the risen Christ in the breaking of the bread. Liturgical archaeologists – of whom I would claim to be but an amateur – are at home in this world, charting the doctrinal shifts in eucharistic theology and peeling away the later medieval accretions with which popular piety and clerical devotion have overlaid the original in an attempt to unearth the pure form of the eucharistic rite of the undivided Church. In this search for an ideal, the basic skeleton has been laid bare by the research of liturgists of all communions, and perhaps the most significant achievement of the ecumenical movement is that the eucharistic rites of most of the Western churches now bear a remarkable similarity. The shape – the skeletal structure – of Order One in *Common Worship* is almost exactly identical to that in the Roman Sacramentary, and to the orders for the Eucharist in the Lutheran, Methodist and Presbyterian churches worldwide.

2 What is said and what is done

Second, there is the raw material of our offering of worship. Along-side the shape of the liturgy there are two elements: what is said and sung, and what is done. The action – the rubrics or the ritual – is often undervalued in our highly verbal, post-Reformation culture. But the action is what makes the Eucharist; 'do this in memory of me' is what Jesus said, and what he is recorded as doing at the end of that Emmaus journey. How we gather, how we attend to what God has to say to us, what we lay on the altar, how we receive commun-ion and what we do as a result is what makes the Eucharist. It is essentially a rite – something done. The words come later, hammered out to express what is happening as each succeeding culture context with its own theological insight seeks to nuance the action, and explain it. But what makes the Eucharist is what is done: that is what guarantees its universality over time and space.

Witnessing the celebration of the sacrament of Baptism in Greece recently, I was struck by the way in which the near continu-ous prayers of the priest, often very repetitive and crammed with biblical and patristic imagery, were hardly listened to in detail by the assembled congregation. They formed little more than an essen-tial drone – the verbal accompaniment to the rich tapestry of the wall paintings on the church, where every square inch was covered in fresco. By contrast, every detail of what was done was watched intently: the priest, followed by the father, blowing away the devil in cross-shaped puffs; the pouring of the oil on the baptismal waters; the oiling of the infant (appropriately named Herakles) for the struggle with the forces of evil ahead like any athlete preparing for the contest; his threefold plunging into the tub, with gasps and flashlights popping as he was raised aloft each time; his being dried off and clothed in the ceremonial white robe, in preparation for his Chrismation as a little prince of the new creation; his being offered the Gospel Book to kiss – the priest carefully taking out his dummy so that he could, and then putting it back in – before being led round the book and the candle in a dance and finally to the Royal Doors to be welcomed to the heaven of which he was now a citizen. At the end of the rite, there was no doubt about what had happened; the meaning of each stage of the drama had been carried not by the texts but by the action.

The other human activity that has always been at the centre of worship is singing. In the Orthodox tradition there is no such thing as a Low Mass, or a quiet service of Holy Communion. You either celebrate the liturgy solemnly or not at all.

On a visit to Georgia, we had set out early from Tbilisi one Sunday morning to see the old fortified abbey of Anuri, and after several hours' drive into the foothills of the Caucasus we arrived at this remote holy place, perched above a lake in a fold of the hills. Imagine my surprise as I approached the church when I heard the sound of Emma Kirkby's voice. The well-known early music soprano is an old friend and her voice is absolutely unmistakable. What was she recording in this lonely place? I tiptoed to the open door and looked in. Of course, it wasn't Emma at all, but a young girl, completely alone in the church and singing ravishingly. Then, from behind the iconostasis came the voice of the priest who was celebrating the liturgy – probably her husband we thought. There were just the two of them in that superb building, except of course for the myriad saints and angels, but the liturgy was still being sung properly, from beginning to end.

Something of this tradition is visible in the charismatic movement where singing is the heart of the offering of worship. And no one who has been to a football match or to a service in Africa would deny the inescapable power of singing to take you out of yourself. This is something that charismatic churches have grasped – that singing is a key element in uniting a community in the offering of the Church's worship.

I believe that this is really important for the Western catholic tradition to grasp as well. Singing together – especially in parts – models the rich harmony of biblical unity rather than the narrow uniformity of a flat unison. That is why I believe in giving people an experience of singing together which everyone can take part in, using music which can be sung confidently after a few moments' rehearsal.

3 Human experience

But third, this is not just a theological pattern; it is also one that is deeply tuned to human experience. The deep structures of human life and longing which the social anthropologists have revealed uncover a pattern of movement and growth which liturgies need to attend to if they are to ring true to human experience and engage with it. Our knowledge of the processes of loss, anger, letting go and bereavement have helped us shape funeral rites – even when the elements have to be compacted into one short act of worship – which are not only rooted in a theology of the movement from death to resurrection, but take account of the stages through which the processes of death and bereavement take us.

Many rites have this 'staged' pattern. The services of Baptism and Confirmation are an obvious example, which again need to recapitulate briefly the long process of conversion, which consists of being drawn into a community, becoming part of its story, finding the security to let yourself be challenged about your past and future, and so come to the baptismal waters at a point in the process when your journey brings you to see the lifetime's pilgrimage which stretches ahead. Baptism is about Spirit-led growth towards maturity within the life of the community of faith as much as it is about an individual's moment of decision. This deep human structure is as important as its liturgical and theological counterparts, and is what enables liturgies to have their power and direction.

4 A sense of order

The other factor I have briefly mentioned in this reflection on the twin peaks in the eucharistic liturgy of Gospel proclamation and the breaking of the bread is order. The liturgy exhibits a pattern and order which reflects something of the divine plan for the cosmos. That order is expressed in how different elements of the liturgy and different gifts within the assembly are related to one another within the whole offering of worship. As individuals, our story is known and valued, but we find our identity before God within a continuing pattern of evolving response to his gift to us. We do not stand alone, and more importantly, we do not sing from our own, individual hymn-sheet.

The pattern of charismatic worship

Although the Eucharist remains the predominant pattern, instituted after all by Christ himself, other patterns of non-sacramental worship have evolved. The pattern of engagement and transformation is also visible in the structured patterns of charismatic worship. These are less obvious to the uninitiated because they do not have a historical pedigree in the same way that the sacraments do. But none the less there is a patterned and understood way of proceeding in the construction of 'a time of worship'.

Fourfold structure

It can often look to the outsider as if there is no particular reason why a series of songs should be placed in the order in which they are in a charismatic 'time of worship'. But there are the same processes at work. Charismatic worship always includes:

1 a song that gathers the community together in worship of God and does its best to articulate some of the community's desires and longings. It moves from this gathering towards
2 a song which says something about the life, the teaching and the ministry of Jesus. Having gathered a community we let God's story be told alongside that of the community. There follows
3 a more highly personal opportunity for engagement with the saving acts of God in Christ: against the backdrop of the larger narrative now comes a much more personal song, attempting to engage the worshipper emotionally with the heart of what Jesus has done for us. This is followed by
4 a song which steps out of this immediate emotional intensity back into a sense of the community's own self-offering. If I have been caught up into Jesus in this particular way, what am I to do or be as a result? This final stage at the end of the sequence of songs points towards action on the part of the believer in witnessing to what God has done for them.

There is a host of worship songs that offer the sense of emotional engagement with what God has done for us in Christ, but it will not always be easy to find the song that articulates the social or political transformation envisaged as a result of drawing close to Jesus. The Pentecostal churches with their origins in the theology of liberation do better: the old spirituals and songs like 'We shall overcome' offer worshippers that sense of realized transformation. So do those paraphrases of the Magnificat like 'Tell out, my soul'. Somehow, turning the vision of our transformed being into the realities of our daily life in meaningful song has not attracted the charismatic songwriters in the same way.

This pattern, which may be filled out to last for a half an hour or more or may be just a compact grouping of songs at the heart of a more recognizably liturgical act of worship, serves to illustrate the same underlying theological structure of the 'liturgy' in the charismatic tradition. But there is also considerable – and growing –

interest in more formal and sacramental liturgical worship that is less at the mercy of its leaders. In 1999 Kingsway Music organized a large conference in Eastbourne to which members of the Liturgical Commission were invited, not only to unpack the way Anglican liturgy worked, but to celebrate with them an Anglican Eucharist. In an assembly attended by a large number of those from House Churches, there was clearly a growing interest in the underlying pattern and shape of liturgical worship, and of the possibility of a liturgy that is nothing more than a series of songs nevertheless having a traditional liturgical pattern and coherence of its own.

It is not always easy for those who are used to the conventions of more traditional liturgy to realize (when sharing in charismatic worship) that although the main elements of liturgical worship are there, these may not be the main structures or carry the main meaning of the act of worship. When I first went to preside at the Eucharist or a Baptism and Confirmation in a charismatic church, I was puzzled by people standing politely by for the key liturgical texts like the Prayer over the Water or even the Eucharistic Prayer, only getting actively engaged when the singing – often of highly subjective and non-biblical texts – started. But then I came to realize that for them the meaning and the engagement were in the singing, not in the 'liturgy', and that the pattern of songs had its own, valid liturgical structure.

A fusion of styles

It will be necessary, if there is to be a proper fusion of these styles, to be able to turn some of the formal liturgy into material that can be set as song, while keeping a certain amount of dialogue between the presiding minister and the assembly; the idea that the assembly should just listen to the presidential Blessing of the Waters in a Baptism rite, for example, is enormously unhelpful in a charismatic setting. What is needed is the translation of such a Prayer over the Water into song, topped and tailed by presidential dialogue and accompanied by presidential gesture certainly, but with the bulk of the telling of the mighty acts of God in the Prayer over the Water being carried by song rather than by spoken presidential text.

Similarly, with the Confession of Faith it may well be possible to use a metric version that is settable within the music culture rather than a long spoken text or even a dialogue between celebrant and assembly. Unless the Church recognizes that this is an important and appropriate option for treating authorized elements of worship, and unless the songwriters in this tradition will work closely with liturgists to provide doctrinally acceptable texts, it is going to be difficult to make progress here. At the moment too many of the texts of worship songs are theologically unadventurous or even worse. They can give the impression of concentrating on the worshippers' feelings and emotions rather than on celebrating what God has done for us and inviting a response. Greater experience of co-operation between songwriters, liturgists and theologians will be important if we are to create the kind of liturgy in which people can both articulate their usual patterns of worship and also find a way in which the beliefs held in the authorized liturgy of the Church of England can actually be made to work in a variety of different contexts.

What we prize in the Anglican tradition is an ordered pattern – a deep liturgical structure that liberates us from the tyranny of the improvising leader – rather than the imposed order that crushes the God-given gifts of the Spirit by leaving no detail unscripted. True spontaneity – like the best musical improvisations – demands disciplined understanding of the deep structures, just as actors are only free to interpret and improvise when they have the text word-perfect. For the Anglican tradition the unity we prize is not a rigid uniformity, a dull unison, but a creative and interactive diversity, a rich harmony. It was sensing that which enabled a child watching a televised service from a cathedral to exclaim: 'Now I know why the churches are true: the people in them enjoy singing and walk about in patterns.'

The shape of other rites

There is a theological shape as well as a liturgical shape to the rites not only of the Eucharist, but of Baptism, Marriage, Funerals and of patterns like vigil rites. All worship worthy of the name models that pattern of engaging and transforming which is at the heart of what God has done for us in Christ in incarnation and redemption. Encounter with the divine Word is never fruitless: 'it will not return to me empty', as God says (Isaiah 55.11, RSV). There is always some change, some movement as we are caught up into 'the upward call of God in Christ Jesus' (Philippians 3.14, RSV) and drawn into the one, perfect self-offering of Christ to the Father.

Liturgies that do not offer worshippers an opportunity to take part in this pattern of encounter and change that leads to growth and development become static and lose their shape and direction. In addition, they fail to engage with our deepest longings and therefore easily remain at the level of spectacle or entertainment: worshippers become spectators as the performance is conducted before them. This is why it is important for those who devise worship to understand the place of each liturgical celebration within the whole drama of our salvation. It is important on Good Friday, for example, to sing the great Passiontide hymn of Venatius Fortunatus, 'Sing, my tongue, the glorious battle', which sets the cross within the whole frame of God's saving activity, and so understands Jesus' death not as a sad end, but, as St John's Gospel (the Passion narrative traditionally read on Good Friday) makes clear, as a triumph. Other hymns like that include 'Of the Father's love begotten' or 'O love, how deep, how broad, how high' or Sydney Carter's 'The Lord of the dance'. In these hymns and songs the whole of our salvation history is laid out, as it is – though very differently – in Bishop Benson's Festival of Nine Lessons and Carols, or in the Baptismal Liturgy of the Easter Vigil. These sweeping liturgies and hymns that set out the whole history of our salvation warn us against liturgies (or theologies) that are bitty, or that fail to set the particular in the context of the whole. In the grand archetypal liturgies, whichever you choose, the underlying sense of movement is the same as we are caught up into the continuing pattern of divine activity.

4 | Telling Our Story

The first thing that happens when the stranger – because he is as yet unknown of course as the Christ – falls in with the companions on the way is not what we might expect. He does not say, 'Hello, I'm Jesus', or 'Don't you recognize me?', or even 'Do you know where I'm going?' His first question – and he seems to appear from nowhere and to be quite happy to walk wherever they are going – is 'Why are you looking so sad?' Anyone who has done any kind of pastoral visit knows that that is just the kind of question to unlock what is biting someone who is miserable. It is just the kind of invitation to open your heart and have the chance of telling your story that so many people long for.

The pilgrimage journey

This telling of your story is of course just what happens on pilgrimage; and not just in Chaucer's time. People have time to talk to one another as they walk together on the way, and so reflect on their own story. How did you come to be here, where did you start from, what is your motivation, what are you hoping for in your life? When we began the pilgrimage walk to Santiago da Compostela at Le Puy and signed in for the journey in the time-honoured way by writing our names in the *Livre d'Or* in the cathedral's sacristy, there was a column to fill in which said (in French) '*motivation*'. So we looked with alarm to see what the person before us had written. She was called Therese and her *motivation* – the spiritual intention of her pilgrimage – was *pour convertir le monde* ('to convert the world'). She came from near Geneva, and we thought at once that we must be following an ardent and serious Protestant. We later caught her up and walked with her and her husband for quite a way. We need not have been alarmed: she was in fact a Swiss Canadian, a Roman Catholic, and more serious than her twinkly husband, Georges, a recently retired telephone engineer. Therese believed that if she had that in her mind and stated it was her aim then her labours in walking would indeed contribute to the conversion of the world. We wrote something rather more domestic, I think – 'to give thanks for 25 years of marriage', which it nearly was. Because since the day when we had been on our honeymoon and had found ourselves in Compostela really by accident on 25 July, St James' Day, we had always had at the back of our minds that one day we would go back, and that this time we would do it properly and walk there as pilgrims.

So ours was a modest kind of *motivation* for a sabbatical. We had the idea that going back to a major place of pilgrimage where we had once been almost unintentionally, and doing it properly this time, would somehow be a rethreading of the beads of life on the string in a rather more robustly spiritual way.

Better examples of motivation among those we met were people who were exploring their vocation, or people whose relationships were in a muddle and wanted to tell you where they were as the means of sorting their own mind out. A lot of people do their thinking as they're telling you their story, because putting it into words in a linear kind of way helps them make the connections they may not have spotted before. I suspect that the world is divided between those who do their thinking with a wet towel around their head locked up in a room on their own and those who do their thinking with other people; and there's a tendency to assume that everyone does their thinking on their own, which our experience does not wholly bear out.

Any invitation to someone to tell their story can be criticized on the grounds that you are making people concentrate on themselves, so becoming more self-centred in the process, which is just the opposite of what you are trying to do in the celebration of the liturgy. But part of the ministry of a deacon (and diaconal ministry is part of a priest's and a bishop's ministry too) is to listen to people's stories and help them tell them as part of day-to-day pastoral work. People who have had a chance to articulate their story know that they have been heard and that they are valued for who they are. When they come to join the eucharistic assembly, they will come with confidence in what they have to offer, and set in relation to God's story.

Our story: penitence and aspiration

There are two things to say about this opening your life and your story to God as part of worship. First, there is the tradition that acts of worship begin with elements of penitence and confession as an essential part of preparation. There is a gut sense that as people are coming together and are conscious of their unworthiness to step over the threshold into the temple or the house of God, this is the moment for ritual cleansing. The fountains in the courtyard before mosques offer the same image, as do holy water stoups or a prominent font with their reminders of baptism near the door of churches. And the practice of reclaiming your baptismal status by making a personal confession too – the one to one – is certainly a preliminary rite. If you are trying to be scrupulously honest about yourself, this may appear to make you concentrate too much on yourself. But the exercise of bringing our story to God and setting it beside God's story, as the disciples did on their walk to Emmaus, is to make you think less about yourself and more about what God is doing and what he's offering and wanting from you.

If our relationship with God is to be truthful, it can only start with the actualities of our lives, not in denying or ignoring them. And just as the disciples on the road to Emmaus had to start by telling Jesus of their disappointed hopes before they could go on to hear what God had done, and how things were being changed even as they walked, so we all need to bring the reality of our story to him. The basis of a newly remade relationship has to be honesty.

The reality of human existence is that we are interested – and properly interested – in ourselves and our relationships, and this is not always to be dismissed as the kind of self-concerned, self-centred part of human nature which is at the root of sin, as some of the more pious spiritual writings assume. An honest look at ourselves is just where we start on Ash Wednesday; it is where we start at the beginning of the liturgy and it is where we start naturally – with the self-concern that the newborn infant expresses when all its energy is concentrated on itself and its needs. But it is not where we ought to remain. Human life is about growing away from that basic self-concern and becoming more aware of others and their needs and more concerned with what God wants his world to be like.

Whether we talk in specifically Christian terms or not, people learn their skills in making relationships and their ability to relate beyond themselves the hard way. Learning social skills – even basic language so that we can communicate – is something we all strive to achieve. You see it in children's early attempts to play together, and by teenage years it becomes the major preoccupation. This natural process starts with small children learning painfully to share their toys and draws us into a world of shared resources and tempered ambitions, all of which enables us – or most of us – to live reasonably contentedly as adults, and at peace with our neighbours. We call it 'growing up'.

Second, there is the aspirational element. The disciples who were walking to Emmaus were not talking about their own sins or shortcomings, but about their hopes and their disappointment. They were sad 'because we had hoped he was to be the one who would redeem Israel'. Their hopes had been built up and now they have been dashed. We do want things to be different but we can't quite make it on our own; or we long to be somewhere else but don't see where the route is lying or where the bridges are, and it is daunting unless anybody has been that way before and blazed the trail.

There are all kinds of elements in our aspirational thinking and longing as well as our acknowledgement of who we are and our concern for ourselves: all this is part of what draws us from who and where we are to where we would want to be, at any rate in our imagination. But can we actually make it to this two-way relationship with God, or is it only a dream?

In the Old Testament Jacob dreams that there is a ladder linking earth to heaven (Genesis 28.1–11). The dream is that there is a way up or a way out of where we are, and that the angels of God go up and down it freely. But it is only a dream. Only in the New Testament does the dream become a reality, where the same picture is used by Jesus in his dialogue with Nathanael whom he calls from under the fig tree. To the astonished Nathanael, Jesus says, 'You will see greater things than these; you will see the heavens opened, and the angels of God ascending and descending upon the Son of Man' (John 1.50–51). In this exchange, John is clearly establishing that while in former times it was only ever a dream that there might one day be a link between earth and heaven, now in Jesus the dream has become reality. Jesus is the ladder that links heaven to earth, and through him we may be drawn up into a relationship with God for real.

So the aspirational element in our lives is not just a pipe-dream. It is all right to dream of heaven, that some day things may be different from how they are at the moment. Aiming for heaven, where we are already citizens, according to St Paul, is our proper end goal. And while none of this absolves us from doing our best to bring about the reality of God's kingdom here and now, earth and heaven are – in Christ – drawn together, and the question becomes, 'How can we become one with Christ?'

A real picture of ourselves

How realistic are we in our assessment of ourselves, or are we often inclined to paint a picture that is distorted by self-pity, or merely self-indulgent? Both of those are possible. There are the people who wallow in their sin and for whom clearly even the recollection of sin is almost lubricious, who feel somehow fed and nourished by the heroic struggle with all this exciting evil that surrounds them with its tentacles. There are also those for whom the experience of knowing that they are entirely locked in themselves is deeply depressing. 'Is it my fault?' Guilt, and especially the kind of self-generated guilt where we somehow think that everything is our responsibility, is even more crippling. You cannot easily escape from it, and the old evangelical technique of labouring your guilt and then preaching for conversion does its best to paint that kind of picture of the human condition into which steps the bright and shining Christ who alone will be able to take you beyond yourself.

It is important not to get too hooked on the liturgical pattern here and think of the self as being merely an endless recital of sinfulness, still less of guilt. Our story can also be a story of disappointment or loss and it can also easily be the story of what has happened to you in a way that you have no control over. So the human story – our story – is not all under the heading of sin and guilt and self-centredness: it is also the story of hopes dashed, of expectations raised and not met and of never quite making it or meeting the goal. That is probably a more common experience for many people. I suspect too that what wears people down is often the circularity of life. You think that you may be getting on a bit better, and lo and behold you suddenly find yourself back where you first started. The schemes we make for self-improvement, whether it's resolutions for giving up smoking or being nicer to the cat, spending more time with the children or driving with more consideration, all tend to end up in dust and ashes and we find ourselves back where we first started. That is quite difficult for people when models of the journey of life are so directional. Paths up mountains are always inviting and full of promise, but then when you have got to the top and seen the promised land you have to come down again. The fact is that our experience of constantly walking around in circles in the fog is much less attractive as a model for life, but actually often feels closer to reality.

Learning to tell your story as it is is actually quite difficult to do, given the culture of concealment, and people's experience of being hurt or taken advantage of. The institutionalized boasting of proud parents (am I the only person to find those Christmas circular letters, purporting to be written by the dog, deeply cringe-making?) can be terribly embarrassing for the children concerned. But it is a rarity in the English culture of natural reticence, and certainly part of my childhood memories was the potential embarrassment of hearing anything about myself, which is certainly one of the reasons why for a long time I was very reluctant to tell anyone anything about myself at all. Telling your story when you know somebody well enough is of course enormously liberating, but it requires a high degree of trust.

Sometimes those people are the confessors or spiritual directors that we adopt in a rather more formal sense. In another way I am struck by how people will tell their stories to complete strangers on occasions when they know it is unlikely that they will ever meet again. It is rather like the anonymity of the confessional. I remember the wife of the head of an Oxford college sitting next to me at a formal dinner telling me a complex and intimate story, and at the end of it breathing a sigh of relief. She probably went away thinking 'I'll never see him again', and indeed she never has. I suspect that could be replicated many times over; people are on the lookout – consciously or not – for safe places. This is why people normally only tell their stories to those whom they love and trust simply because to tell somebody else your story in its entirety is to place yourself entirely in their hands. And there aren't a huge number of people we are ready to do that with. Learning to be honest takes a lifetime and very often it's other people prompting you and stating that they don't think you are being honest with yourself that gives you pause for thought and makes you track back over the story you just told and say, 'Well, was it actually like that, or is that how I wish it had been?' It is quite often difficult – for me, at any rate – to sort reality from imagination.

Encouraging people

What helps people tell their story and what are the skills of the listener who makes people tell their story? In the Emmaus narrative it is the stranger's question, 'Why are you looking so sad?' which turns out to be an effective leading question in this case, though the last thing that makes some people tell their story is having somebody sitting down in the chair opposite them and saying, 'I expect that you want to tell me your story and I hope it will make you feel better.' But Jesus does this on other occasions. He coaxes the Samaritan woman at the well to tell her story, though – as on the Emmaus journey – he knows it already.

The answer must be both a degree of mutual trust, and at the same time the acknowledged forensic abilities of the listener. Helping people piece together a story that has rational connections and logical links is an art that we should cultivate more.

Confession and starting the liturgy

The difficulty about the acts of penitence at the beginning of the Eucharist is that we assume that the confession of sin is the only way – or at least the prime way – in which people want to tell their story, as if what mattered about us is a list of all the things we have done wrong or haven't done that we should have done. The assumption that the human story is the story of human sinfulness isn't particularly helpful to everybody, and is one of the things that people find really difficult about the Christian faith. Do we not allow people to tell their story and celebrate their achievements and their gifts, and are those not a proper part of what needs recognizing as a community assembles for worship? Broken though the human community may be, nonetheless it carries a story of immense perseverance and energy and persistence in the face of every possible kind of discouragement. So when a eucharistic community assembles on Sunday, is a formal confession of sin the best way of opening up their relationship to God's story? No, and indeed what also happens as a community assembles for worship is that they sing hymns of praise as well as chants of penitence. Very often how you choose among the alternatives that shape that part of the liturgy will allow or unlock individual threads which can then be woven into a common mind or purpose.

Sometimes during the course of a week in a local community or church something happens which has a cataclysmic effect and focuses everybody's energy and attention. But quite often it's a question of how different facets of people's experience and what they have been doing and achieving in the week do come together to make some kind of textured whole. People who share the life of a eucharistic community do not only have their own stories as individual people but also generate a common life. What they bring to church to offer in worship is the story of how that community, shaped by its common life and commitment, has engaged with the realities of what has gone on in that place over the past week. And it is not only the immediate past. In many English parish churches there are photographs of former rectors around the walls of the vestry, and names of the people on the war memorials, and books of remembrance, and pictures drawn by the Sunday school last week, and the update on the fundraising for the local hospice, and reminders about Christian Aid Week, and the date of the concert – all significant in forming the background and shape of that particular parish.

At St James', Piccadilly I remember Donald Reeves, the Rector at the time, spending ten minutes at the beginning of the service getting everybody to look around the building and make friends with it, and then looking at each other and telling each other their stories, so that a community – many of them visitors to London – was formed for that particular Eucharist. That was one quite laborious way of doing it, but it did make the point that the community that assembles is a very diverse, fragmented group of individuals which has not only its individual strands of sinfulness and self-centredness but a number of other threads of longings and only partial fulfilments which might be intertwined. If the end result of eucharistic worship is that those strands are woven together in a way that is mutually supporting and enriching as well as giving some kind of strength of purpose to the life of the Church in the future, then giving time to making friends with the building and attending to people's stories is terribly important. Otherwise that experience of attending to who we are and why we are here can so easily be based on make-believe ideas about what people's piety really is, which in the end may not add up to very much when we come to the Dismissal at the other end of the Eucharist. Where's the backbone, who's got the energy, who's got the gifts, what have they brought to church with them that they are ready to offer at the altar to be used and given back, strengthened, intertwined, confirmed and made useful and useable in the service of God's kingdom?

Offering our stories

Liturgically, we can encourage people to bring to church and own all that they hope is going to be used and blessed and given back. That is what the Offertory rites are doing. Although nowadays we only carry up curiously untypical bread and wine, we need to remember that there was a period in the Church when 'making the offering' bore more relation to the reality of people's daily work in the week. As in the barter cultures today, people would have contributed some of what they had made that week rather than cash: the shoemaker some shoes and the baker some loaves. At the end of the liturgy there would have been a distribution rather like you see sometimes in Africa today, where sorting out who needs what takes an enormous time. So there is a sense in which the raw material of our lives can only be given back to us transformed and woven together if we have first been prepared to bring it and own it.

The success of a community in engaging with its neighbourhood will depend very much on what has been drawn to the surface during the week. It is part of the deacon's task to have discovered what has been going on in the week and to make sure that someone is ready to raise it and find the opportunity to articulate it in church: this initial activity complements the deacon's task of sending the community invigorated, restored and transformed out again at the end of the liturgy. For this to be successful, there needs to be conscious attention to this process, and an acknowledgement that this is how the Church's life and liturgy are woven together. It is easy to make theoretical statements about how a community should in theory achieve this kind of organic wholeness, but quite another to make it happen. It is the difference between having services which people attend and being Church.

In his poem, 'The windows', George Herbert captures something of the integral unity of word and action, and his image of God's story being 'annealed' or baked into us like the colours in stained glass so that we shine with God's story, not our own, is a fine image of how doctrine and life are to be one, if the Church is to witness as it should.

Lord, how can man preach thy eternall word?
        He is a brittle crazie glasse:
Yet in thy temple thou dost him afford
        This glorious and transcendent place,
        To be a window, through thy grace.

But when thou dost anneal in glasse thy storie,
        Making thy life to shine within
The holy Preachers; then the light and glorie
        More rev'rend grows, & more doth win
        Which else shows watrish, bleak, & thin.

Doctrine and life, colours and light, in one
        When they combine and mingle, bring
A strong regard and aw: but speech alone
        Doth vanish like a flaring thing,
        And in the eare, not conscience ring.

Reaching beyond ourselves

What gives shape to the business of telling our stories is the aspirational dimension. Why is it that as human beings we are always
trying to reach beyond ourselves and know that there is something
drawing us beyond the horizons of our own immediate vision? Why
is it that we want to test the limits of our endurance, and seek to
reach our potential? Yet we are always conscious of falling short, or
being dragged down by our loss of vision, or our loss of energy at the
end, or our inability to deliver what we aspire to. In the end almost
all of us grow weary. That is part of the natural pattern of human
life – as people draw closer to physical decay and the frailty of old
age we do not have the energy to do all the things we know we
should or would like to. That pattern is replicated in a small way
each day: we start out with good intentions but by late in the day we
actually find it difficult to go on sustaining energy, and opt for
short-cuts and partial solutions in the attempt to overcome what we
know are the limitations of our own energies. Yet we can all surprise
ourselves by how much there seems to be in reserve, when the
adrenalin flows.

That is why companionship in prayer and the Christian life is
important: we get further together than any one of us could on our
own. That is the basic lesson of what it means to be a member of the

body of Christ. That is also where a structured shape to life is important, and why even apparently small things like the shape of the
week are significant. This is more visible in the shape of the liturgical year, with its highs and lows, its feasts and fasts, as well as in the
shape of sacramental celebrations, each one of which encourages us
to be real about ourselves and then reminds us that there is a human
dimension as well to the story of how God in Christ shares our life.
That is why at the heart of Christian worship there are always
readings about God's story, and a disciplined way of telling God's
story by a process of Lectionary readings, which allows little
glimpses, little snapshots into God's story to serve as iconic
reminders of the whole.

Luke's Gospel is particularly good at snapshots, a series of strip
cartoons: his way of telling the Gospel story is particularly suscep-
tible to that kind of treatment. But the telling of God's story is the
subject of the next chapter.

Meanwhile, here is a practical suggestion for better laying out our
story at the start of worship. When will our church communities
have the insight to gather people together either in the hall or at the
back of the church *before* worship rather than after it, so that the
stories of individuals and of the community as a whole can become
part of that essential first stage of laying ourselves before God in
worship? What we need is that sense of engagement with one
another and attention to one another as a preliminary to worship,
rather than as a postlude, when we should be getting on with living
out the Christian life. How are deacons to draw penitential themes
to the surface in the opening rite or to assemble the biddings for
intercession if they only hear afterwards about what has gone on?
How are preachers – especially if they are visiting and therefore
unfamiliar with the details of the community's life over the immediate past (as the bishop nearly always is!) – going to be able to make
the connections in their sermon between God's story and that community's story unless they have some chance of getting the feel of
what are the major concerns of that congregation? I remember once
being told by the incumbent as we were lined up ready to enter the
church that he'd been mulling over in his mind whether to tell me
that the founding father of the new church had died suddenly that
night, so people might be grieving; and – now that he came to think
of it – the organist's wife was dying of cancer, but was determined to
make it to sponsor her confirmation candidate, but that I wasn't to

be surprised if she flaked out; and that the teenager I was about to baptize had just learned that her parents were splitting up. It's information like that that anyone needs if they are to do even a passable job of presiding at worship, let alone preaching in a way that makes the connections for people between what is going on in their lives and what the gospel has to say. Perhaps that is why sermons often seem to work better when there is some national event or agenda, like a war or a death or an election, that everyone has at the top of their minds.

5 | Hearing God's Story of Engaging: Advent to Candlemas

The essential heart of the pattern is this: God in Christ does two things for his people – first he shares their life, then he changes it. These two poles of engaging and transforming not only run through the whole activity of God among his people, but in a particular way undergird all the events which surround the mission and ministry of Jesus.

What lies behind the idea of engaging, of being there: of being with people and working with them, rather than arriving to announce what has been decided and what is going to happen? I think it is simply this: it is the way God worked.

You can view the Old Testament as the record of a thousand years' worth of the Almighty having a shot at telling his people what to do. There are instructions in the Garden of Eden, disobeyed; there are covenants made with Noah by a rainbow, and with Abraham; promises made, and not kept. There are the mighty acts of God in history: the escape out of slavery in Egypt through the waters and the journey through the wilderness to reach the Promised Land. There is the giving of the tablets of stone with the Commandments. All these reveal a picture of God telling his people what to do, knowing that if they are obedient, they will have a happy time of it. Yet the whole of the Old Testament is shot through with their disobedience, with their losing the plot or failing to be gripped by the compelling immediacy of the vision.

It goes on. A period of exile in Babylon does not seem to teach them a lesson; nor did the collapse of the Davidic Kingdom. A series of prophets was either ignored, or if they were speaking the truth too near the bone, were actually shut up, like Jeremiah dumped in the cistern (Jeremiah 38.6). These are all ways in which one can read the story as God trying to tell his people what to do from some distance. But did they listen? They did not, so we can imagine God sighing, and saying to himself: this is no good; nothing works. There's nothing for it but to go in person and talk with them face to face. This is what we see articulated in Jesus' parable in the vineyard (Mark 12.1–12, picking up Isaiah 5.1–7). After the owner had sent servants with messages for the workers in the vineyard about the harvest and the workers had beaten or killed them, the owner says to himself, 'What can I do? I will send my son; surely they will respect him.' So when the Almighty in the end surveyed all these failed attempts to get people to do as they have promised and respond to him, we can imagine him sighing and saying, 'Sending messages won't do: distance diplomacy just doesn't work. There is nothing for it but to go in person. There's no substitute for direct, face-to-face engagement.' This is the force of the opening verses of the Letter to the Hebrews, where the writer says, 'In former times God spoke to us in different ways through the prophets, but in these latter days he has spoken to us by his Son . . .' In these terms, the incarnation, with its looming consequences for the Son, is God's answer to centuries of ever-fraying relationship with his people.

Today we can see the face-to-face pattern being played out in political life. Success comes where people will actually sit down with one another face to face around a table and come to an understanding. This is the only way to build a world community, just as it has always been the way of building a Benedictine community. The Rule of St Benedict tells you to welcome people as if they were Christ himself, and to sit them down and eat with them. The Rule has got the way of building community from the grassroots right, and it is no accident that St Benedict was chosen as the Patron of Europe. Hospitality in that sense has always been one of the key Christian virtues because it is a necessary part of brokering an agreement between different parties. It is difficult for relationships to remain frozen if you sit and eat together, and the re-making of relationships is a key part of the out-working of the incarnation.

At the heart of the incarnation then is this direct encounter. The God of the Hebrews, hidden in the majesty of his remote splendour, where no one may see his face and live, reveals himself in the face of Jesus Christ (see 2 Corinthians 4.5–6). 'In these latter days', says the writer of Hebrews, 'he has spoken to us in his Son.' And that is the force of the directness of the incarnation which is encapsulated in John 1.14: 'The Word was made flesh, and pitched his tent [that is the literal translation of ἐσκήνωσεν, traditionally translated as 'dwelt'] among us.'

The core of the incarnational message is that absolutely direct face-to-face engagement; not hiding behind anything, not sending messages, not remote instructions, but direct, personal encounter. That is of course another reason why, however great a player you may be on the stage of world diplomacy, it does not give the same signals if you sit on an aircraft carrier in the middle of the Indian Ocean and lob your missiles into Afghanistan from a safe distance. It is the face-to-face, hand-to-hand engagement that actually allows you to get the true picture. When you are doing that, you are very much more careful about individual soldiers, especially your own troops, and there is a very different feel to hand-to-hand fighting from blanket bombing, however accurately targeted.

But it is not just in political terms that this style has repercussions. In more domestic situations too people need to communicate. What about the families where children each have their own TVs in their bedrooms as well as their own computers and access to the Internet? What about businesses where person-to-person engagement, even within the firm, is largely through e-mail? What degree of reality does that bring? How many people are concerned that children are growing up with their major friendships being virtual realities rather than real personal engagements?

Incarnation: at the heart of God's nature is the decision to share our life

God's commitment to share our life is the theme of one of the major parts of the Christian year, from Advent to Candlemas. This period, with the celebration of the nativity at its heart, unfolds in liturgical celebration each year the whole range of God's coming among us and taking the risk of sharing our human life.

Advent

The season of Advent, with its pre-Advent Sundays in November at the end of the previous liturgical year, all have the sense of building towards a picture of a world that needs rescuing. The well-known 'Advent' Cantatas of J. S. Bach, like *Wachet Auf* (*Sleepers Wake*) are not in fact Advent cantatas at all; they come from this pre-Advent period when the traditional lectionaries are already pre-echoing what we think of as Advent themes.

It is the celebration of All Saints and the commemoration of All Souls that mark the hinge-point in the liturgical year. They summarize our past and point to our future destiny, alerting us to its uncertainty: are we saints, the comfortably redeemed by our participation in the Paschal triumph; or are we souls, people only a little way on in the process of being changed, as the layers are stripped away by the refining fire of God's love? The modern insertion of the Feast of Christ the King on the Sunday before Advent focuses attention on the great Advent themes of heaven and hell, death and judgement, which people so easily forget in the modern run-up to Christmas which Advent all too often becomes.

There are three Advent themes of 'coming':

- the coming of the kingdom at the end of all things;
- the coming of the kingdom in the particularity of the Christ-child among us;
- the coming of the kingdom among us now, this day, in every moment.

Advent and the pre-Advent season can all be read as operating on these three interlinked layers. The annual keeping of Christmas makes no sense except as an annual preparation for the coming of Christ at the end of all things, with all that goes with the classic Advent themes. People are often surprised to learn that the spine-chilling Dies Irae, which we know as a part of the Requiem Mass, began its liturgical life as an Advent Sequence. In the same way the story told in countless nativity plays and carol services in the annual remembrance of the nativity, the birth of Christ at one time in one place, is – or ought to be – more than a nice fairy story celebrating in a peculiarly nostalgic and English manner the pastness of the past. It ought to sharpen our awareness (how far are we aware?) of the coming of God among us in every moment.

The particularity of Christmas

After the cosmic Advent themes of eternity, Christmas is the point in the Christian year when we are most aware of God's concrete, personal and particular commitment to engagement with time and space and place.

> Welcome, all wonders in one sight!
>   Eternity shut in a span,
> Summer in winter, day in night,
>   Heaven in earth and God in Man;
> Great little one! Whose all embracing birth
> Lifts earth to heaven, stoops heaven to earth.
>   (Richard Crashaw, 1613–1649)

The incarnation is not a generalized event; it takes place in the risky, messy, physical birth of one infant, at one time, in one place. The Christian faith is not a kind of generalized religion with a distant God who stands away and calls us all to fall flat on our faces before him; it is about a call into an immediate, absolutely distinct and very personal relationship. The incarnation marks the major difference between the Christian faith and the other great monotheistic religions of the world.

A relationship that is not one-sided

Framing the Christmas story there is a host of other events. There is the Annunciation to Mary, timed in the liturgical calendar to be nine months before 25 December, when the angel comes and asks the question and the world holds its breath to see if the girl is going to say 'Yes' or 'No'. Mary's 'Yes' is a key part theologically of our whole understanding of the incarnation. God does not force himself on the young girl; the angel comes as a messenger, as an embassy to ask if she will, and we wait to hear what her answer is. The Annunciation emphasizes the manner in which God acts; though he is all-powerful, he does not come bulldozing in, over-ruling and throwing his weight around: he comes patiently waiting, asking, and it requires the 'Yes' of the other. This is an important key to understanding the nature of the relationship between God and his people. God is entering a genuine relationship, not into a pattern of power and obedience where the partners in the relationship are so unequal that it cannot be described as a relationship. This relationship is one of equality: God waits for our yes, he does not force himself on us.

Epiphany: the local map and the worldwide family

Engagement is not just with one family, or one people, who lived in Palestine, at one time, though Jesus will have known the particular contours of that country and known in his time too something of the conflicts which it has so often endured. God in Christ is offering a share of his life to the whole world, throughout all time and over its whole surface. Epiphany is when this small, detailed, particular, single event is suddenly writ large for everyone to see. That absolute particularity of time and place and person that surrounds the incarnation itself is made visible and accessible to all people in all places at all times: this is the meaning of the Epiphany. And that is why at the festival of the Epiphany the manifestation, the making visible of this event is given liturgical expression distinct from that which surrounds the nativity itself: the procession of the magi – the strange figures from distant countries – indicates that we are now witnessing a world event. This King's life is not just a hidden life with personal significance, but is a universal life, which affects people far beyond the borders of Judaea. Matthew's purpose in introducing these strange figures that represent the world order is to make it clear – as in much of the rest of his Gospel – that the significance of this is not merely for those people or for that family or for the whole Jewish people, but for the whole world from one sea's end to the other, as Psalm 72 puts it.

The Baptism of the Lord: Servant and King

In Epiphanytide the themes of the beginning of Jesus' ministry and kingship are also teased out. The Feast of the Baptism of Christ on the first Sunday of the Epiphany reminds us that Christ's public ministry is inaugurated at his baptism. This baptism is both submission to the waters (entering into servanthood) and being raised out of the waters (anointed with the Holy Spirit). The voice that declares Jesus' divine Sonship quotes from two Old Testament passages – a coronation psalm pointing to Jesus as King (Psalm 2.7) and one of the Servant Songs of Second Isaiah (Isaiah 42.1) revealing that this anointed king is also going to suffer for his people.

These will be among the prophetic texts that Jesus will have explained to his disciples on the way to Emmaus, when Luke says 'he interpreted to them in all the scriptures the things concerning himself' (Luke 24.27, RSV). In our baptism into Christ's body, we are drawn into the royal, priestly character, but are also told that the way this divine character will become ours is by being drawn into his pattern of self-sacrifice and suffering.

This is how Christ's body continues. The divine light is not confined to one person whose earthly life ended 2,000 years ago, but is handed on to each baptized Christian. The Epiphany season is the celebration of that explosion of light. Each tiny individual pinprick of flame – the life and virtues of each Christian disciple – adds up to a worldwide blaze. When the newly baptized are sent out of church at the end of the Baptism service, they are given a candle with the words: 'Receive this light . . . Shine as a light in the world . . .'

Candlemas: Christ, the Light of the World

The Epiphany season ends with Candlemas, celebrating the moment when Christ was recognized by Simeon, the old priest in the temple, as the light of the world. It is in the temple at Jerusalem, the heart of established Jewish worship, that Jesus is recognized by a member of the priestly tribe as the light of all the nations, not just of the chosen people. Again, a particular domestic event comes to have universal significance: the family comes to fulfil their ritual obligation of redeeming the first-born who is offered to God, and the old priest in the temple recognizes the infant as the Christ, and says that this is what the world has been waiting for.

God continues to engage with his people to this day. As people respond to his story, his vision, his promise, his call, we today can share in that purposeful sense of his direct engagement with us.

Forming the pattern in us

This pattern of the incarnation is formed in us by our keeping of Advent, Christmas, Epiphany and Candlemas in the annual liturgical celebration of the Church's year. But there are other ways in which we reinforce the pattern of engagement in our lives.

First, there is the call of baptism where God speaks to us directly. It is his call that we respond to. In Isaiah 43.1 God says to his people: 'I have called you by name, you are mine' (RSV). Words that derive from these are used by the bishop when he addresses the candidates as he confirms them: 'Tom, God has called you by name and made you his own.' Yet we only hear that call when we are alert to the demands made on us to look up and out from our self-absorption. Unless we acknowledge that our story is unfinished, we do not recognize the call of God as being addressed to us. But when we respond to that call, the transforming love of God incorporates us into the divine life, to share God's responsibility for caring for his created order. Baptism is not only about making churchgoing

Christians: it is about drawing us into God's continuing care for the whole world, so that as we are made members of his royal priestly people, we take up our responsibility as his regents and viceroys on earth to care for it and for his people, as he cares for us. In the call to be baptized, the shape of the incarnation is visible.

Second, there is the ministry of preaching. While it is the preacher's task to relate God's story to our story and help people recognize how one challenges the other, it is important to recognize that within each sermon, the pattern of the incarnation is being rehearsed. The Advent call to look up and out for the signs of what God is doing is what prepares us for the vivid particularity of God's coming among us, and the personal challenge of his presence. In a sermon, the preacher has the task of discerning the signs of God's activity in the ordinary things of life, and then helping the hearers to recognize how that challenges them to engage with what God is doing.

Third, the pattern of the incarnation is rehearsed in the pattern of daily prayer in the Church. Just as there is a weekly shape to the Church's worship, focused on the sacramental celebration of our redemption with every Thursday evening echoing the Last Supper, every Friday being a mini Good Friday, every Saturday a *dies non* as the Lord lies in the tomb and creation keeps its Sabbath rest, and every Sunday with its celebration of the Eucharist a weekly celebration of the resurrection (see Chapter 6), so the pattern of the celebration of the incarnation is rehearsed each day.

The shape of our days

We can see the incarnational shape of the day if we look at the four canticles from Luke's Gospel (Luke 1.28–30; 1.46–55; 1.68–79; 2.29–32) that we know as the Angelic Salutation, the Magnificat, the Benedictus and the Nunc Dimittis. These Gospel canticles form the climax of the traditional fourfold prayer of the Church at morning, mid-day, early evening and late night – Morning Prayer, Mid-day Prayer, Evening Prayer and Night Prayer – or as we used to call them: Matins, the Angelus, Evensong and Compline.

Morning: preparing to recognize the signs of God's kingdom
Morning Prayer at the start of the day looks forward with an Advent longing to recognize the sign of God's coming among us. The

Benedictus rehearses the way in which God comes to deliver us, alerting the worshippers to wake up, and look upwards and outwards to what God is doing to bring in his kingdom.

> Blessèd be the Lord the God of Israel,
> who has come to his people and set them free.
> He has raised up for us a mighty Saviour,
> born of the house of his servant David . . .
> Free to worship him without fear,
> holy and righteous in his sight all the days of our life.
>
> In the tender compassion of our God
> the dawn from on high shall break upon us,
> To shine on those who dwell in darkness and the
>   shadow of death,
> and to guide our feet into the way of peace.
>
> (*Common Worship*)

Those who say Morning Prayer and recite the Benedictus day by day are having their antennae sharpened so that when they step out into the new world of the coming day, they are all ready to see the signs of God's kingdom and to acknowledge its presence. If you go out expecting to see God active in his world, the chances are you may spot what he is doing and be ready to co-operate with it. That's the hope, at any rate, and it has been the tradition of the Church that at Morning Prayer you are not just looking back to the one historic event of the coming of Christ foretold by John the Baptist, but you are actually tuning yourself to recognize the signs of his presence and so be able not just to cluster round and celebrate it, but help draw others into making the kingdom actually happen.

But do we recognize the signs of God's coming among us? For all our praying the Benedictus, do we spot the signs of the kingdom? Are we alert to those acts of power which we are being invited to co-operate with or turn into reality when we get the chance, or do they pass us by?

Mid-day: the tap of the angel

That depends on whether we are alert to the message of the angel. Do you recognize what's happening when the angel taps you on the shoulder and says, 'Hey, I've got something for you to do'? Do you

stop what you are doing and say, 'Yes, let me lend a hand to that'?
Quite often I think we don't; we say, 'Oh, do go away; I'm terribly
busy about the Lord's business: I'm writing next Sunday's sermon',
or 'I'm praying', or 'I've got a meeting', when actually what we are
being asked is to take part in making the kingdom happen now.
How often does the angel tap you on the shoulder? A couple of
times an hour, once a morning, once a week, once a lifetime? How
do we recognize the moment when it comes? How do we practise
saying 'Yes'?

We need to practise saying 'Yes' to the tap of the angel by patterning ourselves to respond to God's call positively, whenever it comes,
like Mary. God's presence with us is visible in the particular, in the
small particulars of life. Recognizing this was what the shepherds
did at the nativity, and the mid-day focus on the particularity of
Christ's presence among his people is what the Angelic Salutation or
Angelus does. We tend to think of the Angelus through the eyes of
the pre-Raphaelite painters (both French and English) whose paintings are full of romantic pastoral scenes where, when the bells ring
at noon in the distant church tower, people lean piously on their
scythes and pruning hooks looking reverential, though really they
are waiting to hurry off to dinner. But actually the point of saying
the Angelus at noon (or whenever it is) is to have a moment in the
day when you consciously practise for what is going on all the time
by using the Angelic Salutation.

> The angel of the Lord brought tidings to Mary,
> and she conceived by the Holy Spirit.

That is how it begins, and we reply with first the angel's words, and
then Mary's cousin Elizabeth's:

> Hail Mary full of Grace, the Lord is with you.
> Blessed are you among women,
> and blessed is the fruit of your womb, Jesus.

And so it goes on, with Mary's 'Yes':

> Behold, the handmaid of the Lord;
> Let it be to me according to your word.

And then the heart of the incarnation itself:

The Word was made flesh, and dwelt among us.

All those key sentences which rehearse the to and fro that leads to the incarnation are in the dialogue, with the repeated prayer of the Angelic Salutation:

Hail Mary full of Grace, the Lord is with you.
Blessed are you among women,
and blessed is the fruit of your womb, Jesus.

The Angelus finishes with the prayer that we know as the Collect for the Feast of the Annunciation, where we pray 'that as we have known the incarnation of your Son Jesus Christ by the message of the angel, so by his cross and passion we may be brought to the glory of his resurrection'. At the nucleus of the Collect is the movement that links the incarnation forward to death and resurrection. Every moment we say 'Yes' to the angel's call, we are entering the fray for the victory of life over death, to help make good triumph over evil.

Evening: have we helped God to turn the world upside down today?

At Evening Prayer, the Gospel canticle is the Magnificat, the Song of Mary, and echoing the Epiphany, we cheerfully sing of God's universally acclaimed action:

He has put down the mighty from their seats,
and exalted the humble and lowly;
He has filled the hungry with good things
and the rich he has sent empty away.

There is always a challenge in singing those words. Yes, God may have done that once so that Mary could sing of it; but has it happened today? What have I done about it? When I saw the high and mighty did I help topple them off their thrones? When I saw the hungry, did I feed them? So there is always a challenge in the Magnificat as we broadcast the triumphs of God in turning the world upside down, and rejoice in the topsy-turvy values of the kingdom and their demands. Have we ourselves been involved in making it happen? Or is the Magnificat a rather salutary reminder that perhaps we haven't taken all the opportunities we could?

That is why there tends to be a slightly retrospective feel about Evening Prayer, and a trace of personal penitence as well as praise. Is there anything about the day that we want to bring before God in terms of missed opportunities, or ones that we simply didn't recognize? The recital of the Magnificat, the Gospel canticle for Evening Prayer, will always challenge our commitment to the values of God's kingdom.

Night Prayer: signing off and handing over

As we come to the time to go to bed at the end of the day, we pause to rejoice in what God has done, whether recognized by us at the time or not, and to let go of the day. The silver of the dawn has passed from the blaze of pure light at noonday through the gold of the evening, and now the velvet of night has come. Like old Simeon in the temple who at the end of his life held the infant Christ in his arms for a moment and recognized him as the long-awaited Light of the World, we are ready to sign off. But we do it cheerfully, not because we think we have made a good fist of handing it on to others so that the light will shine on in the darkness whether we are there or not. Guarding the flame of the gospel and the success of the Christian faith does not depend entirely on us. We are a great part of a continuing chain, both historically and worldwide, of prayer and witness, but it is not all up to us. When the hymn, 'The day thou gavest, Lord, is ended' says:

> As o'er each continent and island
> The dawn brings on another day;
> The voice of prayer is never silent,
> Nor dies the strain of praise away

it is pointing to the continuity of the Church's prayer through time and space, to the fact that Christ is the King of all times and places, and that it is all right to surrender the baton at the end of the day and say, 'Lord, I have done my best for you this day in cherishing your light and helping people see, but now I am going to sleep, because if I don't, I won't be any good in the morning.' I can do this cheerfully because I know that others are carrying the torch through the night; it is always dawn somewhere in that moment, and some-where communities will be offering the Eucharist in that moment as in any other, right through each night and day.

The hand-over of old Simeon in the Nunc Dimittis is maintained by the way the Church hands on its mission from person to person as the world sinks into night on one side of the globe and springs into light on the other. The sense of absolute continuity in the sacrificial offering of praise and worship is maintained, but it is not dependent on us.

The order for Night Prayer or Compline remains exactly the same day by day throughout the year, save for some Alleluias in Easter-tide. This is because as the final monastic office of the day, Compline was said as the monks stood by their beds in the dark dormitory, ready to go to sleep. Compline signs off for the night, and the tradition of knowing it by heart is worth perpetuating. In particular, it is good to learn the three verses of the Nunc Dimittis. Even if you say no more of Night Prayer each evening, the Nunc Dimittis will round off the day, and bring the daily incarnational cycle to a conclusion, after travelling through the day from Advent to Candlemas.

6 | The Love of God Transforms Us: Lent and Easter

What is transformation?

Transformation is what happens in a charged moment when the spark jumps between two points that are close but not touching, as in a sparking-plug in a car. In the Emmaus narrative, the first of these two points is the tale told by the dejected disciples as they walk away from Jerusalem, of how all their hopes and dreams had turned to dust; and the second is the exegesis given by the stranger who fell in with them, of how God had prepared his people for a Messiah who would enter into his glory through suffering. In both their account and his exposition there is a story of mounting disaster. But the disciples do not see the parallels. They do not make the connections between their experience and his story. No spark jumps.

If they had reflected on their history more, as we might have expected at Passover time, they would have been better prepared. The waters of the Red Sea are waters that drown, but actually they provided a way of escape from Pharaoh's pursuing army. In the exile into Babylon – it was an utter disaster to lose your homeland and the temple and the nation's entire identity that was so bound up with the land – the place of exile and despair was discovered to be a place in which community becomes real, and longing for God becomes invigorating and purifying once again. But in spite of the repeated history – Abraham and Isaac, Noah, Jonah, the burning fiery furnace and a whole host more – the disciples do not see it.

Then the stranger takes the bread, blesses and breaks it, and suddenly the spark jumps. Their eyes are opened and the pieces click into place. What connects the experience of those disciples who walked to Emmaus – their frustrated hopes and unfulfilled longings – with the ancient story of God's people – the escape from slavery in Egypt and their restoration from exile in Babylon – is the figure who mysteriously stands before them. He has set God's story against theirs, but without the thread of recognition the penny did not drop.

But now, when at table he takes the bread, says the blessing, and then breaks it and gives it to them, their eyes are opened. What enables them to connect their present experience and all his exposition of what the scriptures foretold about him – the spark that jumps when he breaks the bread before them – is that the stranger repeats those very same acts that Jesus had done at that Last Supper. What they suddenly realize is the connection between the events in the upper room when Jesus took bread, blessed and broke it, and then uttered the strange words, 'Take, eat, this is my body which is given for you; do this in remembrance of me' and his death on the cross the next day. Now they grasp that his death was foretold in the breaking of bread at the Last Supper, and when they see that bread being broken before their eyes, they recognize that the one whom they had thought was dead, his body broken on the cross, is now alive in their midst.

The spark today

Where does the spark fly today, and how can it jump for us? We cannot make it happen; we can only prepare for it and create the conditions that will make it possible. The kind of spark that flies across between two apparently unconnected points, God's story and ours, and transforms our vision, is not of our own making; it is essentially God's doing.

The celebration of each sacrament offers a moment when our longing for transformation is met by God's gift of grace. We will explore that further in Chapter 10 when considering the sacraments. But the pattern of transformation, the opportunity for the spark to fly, is seen most clearly in the celebration of Lent, Holy Week and Easter, in the period between Ash Wednesday and Pentecost.

The redemption cycle

The incarnation cycle, the celebration from pre-Advent onwards through Christmas and Epiphany, finishes at Candlemas. And then the Church's year has a fallow period until the start of Lent – sometimes it is a very short period indeed if Easter is early. The next cycle starts with Ash Wednesday and runs from there through Lent, through the celebration of the Great Week to Easter, and right through Eastertide and the Ascension to Pentecost, the fiftieth and final day of Easter.

In this cycle the momentum is quite different. The momentum here is not that of a gradual revelation of the light, a gradual unfolding, of eyes being prepared in the dark to see the particularity of the living flame and then the sense of that light's universal spreading. It does not have that kind of still moment at the centre focused on the celebration of the incarnation at Christmas; there is no contraction of our broad vision into a pinprick of light from which it then expands again. In the Paschal cycle there is much more of a story-line, a linear pattern of development. In a series of events offering a series of opportunities for transformation, we start from the enormous pain and suffering of the world and its need for redemption – our need for change, for rescue from our selfish selves. Lent as a time of serious rehearsal for turning away from sin and turning to Christ continues to involve us in growing, in a daily transformation and renewal. The events of Holy Week draw us into many experiences of change and transformation, from the euphoric welcome to Jesus as he rides into Jerusalem, to his betrayal by his own disciples as well as the crowds; from the breaking of the bread at the Last Supper, to the transforming recognition by the disciples at Emmaus; from the death which is transformed into victory, from the isolation of our weak discipleship, to the complete overthrow of all fears by the resurrection.

Ash Wednesday

The annual celebration of our redemption starts with Ash Wednesday. At the centre of the liturgy on that day, as people receive the imposition of ashes on their forehead, is the chilling reminder, 'Remember you are dust and to dust you shall return.' Those are words from Genesis, from the dialogue between God and the woman in the garden, when the slimy serpent loses its limbs and bites the dust.

It is hard to make sense of such a put-down when we are trying to build up people's sense of self-worth and dignity. Are we not made in the image and likeness of God? But unless we are realistic about the starting point, our relationship with God will be built on shaky foundations. In spite of our unworthiness, God has chosen and formed us for himself, and loves us. That is why being realistic about our story is essential before we set it against God's story.

Lent

From that moment on, the journey through Lent picks up the journey of the wilderness, the wandering in the desert in Old Testament terms echoed by the wilderness years for the Christ. Not just the temptations in the wilderness, but the whole of the wilderness years, the whole of the hidden period before Jesus' baptism and the start of his ministry.

> Lent got its original shape from being the period of immediate preparation for those who were ready to renounce their old ways and follow Christ, and were to be candidates for baptism at Easter. During Lent the candidates renounced their old life in stages, and prepared for the new life with which they would be clothed at Easter. These days we use Lent similarly, as a period for spring-cleaning our spiritual lives, so that when we come to the celebration of Holy Week and Easter we are ready to enter again with Christ into death to self and sin that we may rise to new life in him. People think of Lent as a time to give things up, to escape from the tyranny of personal over-indulgence and institutional clutter, but the point of doing that is to enable growth to take place. And anyway, between winter and spring is the time to prune so that the new growth will be fresh and strong. Training ourselves to expect growth is one of the ways in which we prepare for Easter's sharp demands for a sudden and radical change.

Holy Week

Lent is followed by the celebration of Holy Week which adds to the linear feel of the story of our redemption, in the way we have come to celebrate the events of Christ's passion in a historical sequence.

> Of all the Gospel writers it is Luke who has the strongest linear narrative sense. His Gospel can be read rather like a strip cartoon – as a series of vivid vignettes which unfold the story by engaging people in it scene by scene, as if they were bystanders. The Emmaus story – unique to Luke – is not the only example. There is the Prodigal Son and the Good Samaritan. And where would we be at Christmastime without Luke? It is in Luke that we find the most developed infancy narratives.

In celebrating Holy Week, the Church has developed a way of re-enacting these events in the liturgy as if they were happening now. This has given people a way of entering into them dramatically and identifying with them by engaging worshippers as participants to a greater extent than at other times in the Church's year.

We can see how this developed from quite an early stage, because we have Egeria's diary. This fourth-century Spanish nun was the first pilgrim to the holy places in Jerusalem who kept a diary that has survived, and it is from her that we know how Holy Week was celebrated in those days. A series of dramatic celebrations, following the pattern of the Gospel, took place as far as possible on the sites where the original events took place and were accompanied by the appropriate readings.

Palm Sunday

She tells, for example, how the Christian community gathered at Bethany outside Jerusalem, read the account of Palm Sunday from the Gospel and walked into Jerusalem carrying olive branches as a vivid re-enactment of Jesus' triumphal entry, much as we do today in gathering the community outside the church and then processing in to start the celebrations of Holy Week, making the church our Jerusalem for the week.

In Holy Week the liturgies often deliver sharp contrasts. By identifying with the sharp mood-swings of the crowd we learn a lot about how shallow our own allegiances are. The Palm Sunday procession, with its shouts of triumph and its optimism about Christ's kingship, has the crowd who have sung 'Hosanna' shouting 'Crucify him!' only half an hour or so later, as they take the part of the bystanders in a dramatic reading of the Passion. People's awareness that within half an hour they have been swept along with the crowd and shifted from cheering the hero of the moment to calling for his head is what the liturgical drama offers them: the experience of change, only this time – as so often – not a change for the better.

Taking part in the whole of the Holy Week liturgy offers this experience of change, of the movement from light to darkness and then back again, from the dust and ashes of Ash Wednesday to the body glorious, from death to life. Many of the liturgies – not just that of the Easter Vigil – have the seeds of that change within them, even if you need to take part in the whole cycle to appreciate it fully.

Maundy Thursday

Maundy Thursday centres on the various events surrounding the Last Supper as the Church celebrates the inauguration of the Eucharist. That evening, the celebration includes a dramatic representation of the Gospel (John 13.1–15) when the presiding celebrant washes the feet of members of the congregation, making visible the new commandment of loving service and enrolling them, like Peter, in Jesus' continuing ministry. At the end of the liturgy, the sacrament from which communion will be given tomorrow is carried to an altar where a Watch is kept, giving us an opportunity to 'watch and pray' with Jesus in the Garden of Gethsemane, while the rest of the church is stripped of its furnishings as Christ was stripped of the companionship of his friends and prophetic psalms (22 and 55) are read. All these events are telescoped together into one liturgical observance. That is how the liturgy often works. It recalls in a quite brief span of an hour or two's liturgical commemoration a whole series of stages in the process through which a community has travelled.

Good Friday

While popular devotion – whether the Jesuit-inspired Three Hours' Devotion or the Stations of the Cross – concentrates on identifying with the sufferings of Jesus, the formal liturgy of Good Friday celebrates the triumph of the cross. The Gospel is always the Passion according to John, where the cross is seen as the moment where God's glory is revealed, and the whole world is drawn to worship at the foot of the cross: 'I, if I am lifted up, will draw all people to myself' (John 12.32).

This triumph is announced in Jesus' dying words – 'It is finished', or, more accurately: 'It is perfectly accomplished.' So in the liturgy, after the reading of the Passion, the cross is carried in, raised three times with a triumphant acclamation, and set up for veneration. It was Helena's discovery of the beams of the cross itself – rather nicely called 'the Invention of the Cross' in the old calendar – that drew Egeria and millions of others in her wake to Jerusalem. 'These events were real: look, here is the actual wood', was the message, and you will feel some of that as you step forward in the Good Friday liturgy in your parish church and lay your head for a moment on the wood of the cross as the Reproaches are sung, those ancient texts whose traditional music owes more to Constantinople than to Rome.

The Easter Vigil

The drama of these celebrations culminates in the Easter Vigil where worshippers are offered the actual experience of change, of stepping out of the dark and into the light, out of the old and into the new.

> Any of the baptismal images are appropriate for this experience, whether they are baptismal images of death and resurrection or of being unclothed and further clothed, or of being newborn into a new life in which you grow and through which you come to maturity.

At the Easter Vigil the congregation assembles in the dark – either late on the Saturday night or in the darkness of pre-dawn – to experience the sense of radical change that resurrection brings. In the darkness, prophetic readings from the Old Testament include some of the great stories of God's deliverance, beginning with the opening verses of Genesis, where light is created out of the watery darkness.

> These narratives include the Creation and Fall (Genesis chapters 1—3), the rescue of Noah and the rainbow covenant (Genesis 6.11—9.17), God's testing of Abraham and the covenant that followed it (Genesis 22.1–18), a good deal of the narrative surrounding the Exodus, beginning with God's appearance at the burning bush (Exodus 3.1–15) and leading through the account of the plagues in Egypt (Exodus 5.1–22) to the Passover (Exodus 12.1–24). Most significant is the story of the rescue of the people of Israel through the waters of the Red Sea (Exodus 14.15–31).
>
> The readings may also include the account of Joshua's entry into the Promised Land (Joshua 1.1–9), the rescue of the Three from the burning fiery furnace (Daniel 3), much of the book of Jonah, with God's rescue of Jonah from the belly of the great fish (Jonah 1.1—2.10) and Ezekiel's prophetic parable of the valley of the dried bones (Ezekiel 37.1–14).

People may be sitting around a bonfire, or a charcoal brazier; but this moment is one of the few times in the year when, mesmerized by the firelight, people can manage to listen to long biblical stories. Then as the dying embers dwindle into darkness, the Easter candle is marked, blessed and lit from the embers of the fire with the words 'May the light of Christ, rising in glory, banish all darkness from our hearts and minds.' The candle is carried through the church, and raised – like the cross three days before – with the triumphant acclamation, 'The Light of Christ', before the great Easter proclamation is sung.

Then, as the resurrection is announced, gongs, bells, organs and other instruments sound, and to those who have never experienced it before, this sharp moment when darkness gives way to light, silence to deafening sound and death to life, is electrifying. In the darkness of the night, says St Matthew, there was an earthquake and from within the tomb new life burst out, trampling down the gates of hell and unlocking the prisoners of death.

In a church now ablaze with light, the baptismal candidates are asked to turn west and renounce the powers of evil and then east to declare their allegiance to Christ. After the Alleluias and the Gospel they are brought to the font where they are baptized into Christ's death by going down into the dark waters and being raised to new life. Cyril of Jerusalem, speaking to candidates later about their baptism, asks them to think back to that moment:

> When you went down into the water it was like night and you could see nothing; but when you came up again it was like finding yourself in the day. That one moment was your death and your birth; that saving water was both your grave and your mother.
>
> (Mystagogical Catecheses II.4)

When the candidates have been kept back in the darkness of a narthex or porch, and only step into the illuminated church through the waters of baptism, this sense of entering a new world is powerfully expressed for them. They are then clothed, anointed and welcomed into the life of the Church with the words:

> May God, who has anointed you by baptism into his Church,
> pour upon you the riches of his grace,
> that within the company of Christ's pilgrim people
> you may daily be renewed by his anointing spirit,
> and come to the inheritance of the saints in glory.

That prayer reinforces for the candidates the pilgrim journey into which they have entered, and in which they will continue in the company of the Church, living and departed, for the rest of their lives. It is that sense of journey, of movement through a building, of moving through the stages in their life, that is most powerfully expressed at the Easter Vigil, and indeed throughout this whole season from Ash Wednesday to Pentecost.

> It would be possible to express the unity of the whole season by celebrating a baptism in stages. If you renounce the powers of darkness and promise to follow Christ on the first Sunday in Lent, you would be signed with the cross and receive the badge of Christian pilgrimage in company with others who had enrolled for Lent on Ash Wednesday. Then at the Easter Vigil, you declare your faith in the risen Christ, and are baptized into Christ's death and resurrection, being anointed and admitted to communion. Finally, at Pentecost you receive a charge to live the Christian life, being sent out to live and work as Christ's disciple, bearing your candle lit from the Paschal candle as a sign that the resurrection life is now handed over to each member of the Church to be lived.

The Ascension

In the early Church the whole of the celebration of death and resurrection, including Good Friday, the Ascension and Pentecost, was celebrated in that one night's liturgy. That is certainly true to St John's theology, where on the cross Jesus is lifted up for the world's adoration and hands over his spirit to the nuclear Church, his mother and the beloved disciple. Then on the day of resurrection, he appears among the disciples and gives them their apostolic charge, breathing over them and saying, 'Receive the Holy Spirit.'

Later, following the Lukan strip-cartoon tradition, the events were historicized, and each given a distinct emphasis. The Ascension and Pentecost were celebrated as distinct moments, enabling people to enter the events of the drama one by one. This is the linear pattern that has characterized the Church's whole celebration of the transforming drama of the redemption.

The reversal of our Ash Wednesday experience of being nothing but dust before the majesty of God is what Ascension Day promises. Now the threads of gold in our being are sifted from the dross and dust, and our human nature is caught up in Jesus' being reunited with the Father, his work being crowned with success. In him, we too are raised to the very throne of God. Bishop Christopher Wordsworth spells this amazing truth out in a remarkable Ascension hymn:

Thou hast raised our human nature
  in the clouds to God's right hand;
There we sit in heavenly places,
  there with thee in glory stand;
Jesus reigns, adored by angels;
  man with God is on the throne;
Mighty Lord, in thine ascension
  we by faith behold our own.

Pentecost

At the end of this cycle of the celebration of our redemption comes Pentecost. This is the moment that marks the outward thrust of the energy generated by the risen life. No longer were the disciples waiting around for someone else to do something; like the disciples at the supper table in Emmaus, they realized that if anything was going to happen, it would be because they took matters into their own hands, and this was just what God intended. Liturgically, Pentecost often seems a bit tame, just as the Dismissal rites at the end of the Eucharist seem pretty thin. Often the only drama in the service is the blowing out of the Paschal candle! This is a good opportunity to renew the apostolic charge to live out the Christian life, and at least make sure that the single flame of Easter is actually dispersed effectively in ways that count. Is this the moment in the year to charge the congregation with a renewed commitment to mission?

The radical change of transformation

All these celebrations have *radical change* at their core, even if some express it more gradually than others. The essential movement from Lent to Easter is the movement of 1 Peter 2.9: 'God has called us out of darkness into his marvellous light.' The drawing of Christians on their journey of faith into that journey, celebrated each year between Ash Wednesday and Pentecost, which is essentially the journey of Christ through his Passion and death to risen life with his relationship with the Father restored, is the essential movement of our prayer in the crucified, risen and ascended Christ.

Making the connection

The Emmaus disciples' dispiriting experience and the ancient story of God's people are connected by the figure who is now sitting with them, and what he did only a few nights back sparks into life to connect the two. At the time of the Last Supper they had not understood the references he was making. There they were, in the context of the Passover celebrating the great escape, the rescue of God's people from slavery and the great liberation cry for freedom, yet the next day had seemed to be nothing more than an end and a death.

Now, in a flash they see that that break-point of the crucifixion was the opening up of a new future. Jesus had taught that this is the natural way of growth and new life, as in John 12.24: 'Unless a grain of wheat falls on the earth and dies, it remains alone' (RSV), and if it's enclosed in its husk it can't break out; but as soon as the damp and the warmth of the soil get into it, then the natural processes can start and then the grain can expand and the root grow to produce an enormous crop.

At the Passover the unleavened bread is broken and the jagged pieces are laid on the table as a sign that the meal can begin. With Jewish practicality the housewife has been around ritually with a feather duster and swept up all the crumbs before the Passover begins in order that not a crumb of the old shall remain, and a clean break with the musty old leaven be achieved and a fresh start made. A new community is forming and new life is coming into being. So, in the Paschal action of the Eucharist, a new creation is being formed; the world is being transformed and our redemption celebrated.

Our experience of transformation now

That has been the Church's continuing experience. The touchstone of our experience of transformation, the yardstick by which we measure everything else, is the celebration of the Eucharist. Each Eucharist rehearses the whole event of God's sharing our life in Jesus and then changing it. And as the Eucharist celebrates it and we reflect on it, this experience of recognition, of the transforming jump, becomes a continuous focus for all our other momentary recognitions and tiny glimpses.

Each time we celebrate the Eucharist we are celebrating all of the elements of God's engaging with us and transforming our life which Luke teased out into separate scenes: the Advent expectation in the community's gathering and preparation; God's coming among us in the

Word made flesh each time the Gospel is proclaimed in our midst; the Epiphany-like spelling out of this in the sermon as good news for the whole world now; Christ's ministry of concern and healing as we bring our intercession into conformity with his prayer to the Father; our triumphal entry with him into Jerusalem as we move to the altar with our gifts – the Great Entrance, the Orthodox call it; our thanksgiving to the Father for our creation, redemption and all the blessings of this life in the Eucharistic Prayer, as we recall Christ's command to 'do this' in memory of him at the Last Supper; the mystery of Christ's self-giving death on the cross as the bread is broken; the moment of our Easter as we who receive the broken bread – that sign of death – into our hands, are made whole and one again in communion with him; and the prayer that a renewed community will go out to transform the world, which provides a mini-Pentecost in the Blessing and Dismissal at the end of each celebration.

Christ is known in the breaking of the bread. That is the phrase that runs through Luke 24 and is picked up in Acts 2.43–47, and becomes the earliest name for the Eucharist. The other moments of change and recognition are given meaning by this supreme moment: those spark-points across which the connections are made between the eternal, archetypal stories of God's dealing with his people and individual Christians' actual experience held in the Church's continuing memory, as they are handed on from person to person in the continuous sacramental life of the Church – those spark-moments hold the key. Whether it is the breaking of the bread, or the moment when the candidate's forehead is inscribed with the cross or their head is pushed beneath the waters, or hands are joined in marriage: these individual spark-points connect with other parts of the same story, and weld our life to God's.

At the heart of every sacramental experience of the Church is a moment of disjunction and conjunction. There is always a death and resurrection. A sacramental celebration involves a radical change, a death to a past state, before a new life emerges, such as we can see in Baptism and Confirmation, in Marriage, in Reconciliation, in Healing, and in Ordination. A sacrament offers a moment in which this changed quality of relationship between people or within a community is signalled; where suddenly distinctiveness or individuality is experienced not as a sign of disunity but the raw material for a deeper kind of complementarity.

That moment of disjunction and conjunction is part of the Pentecost experience, which involves the radical reversal of the Tower of Babel. In the story of Babel (Genesis 11.1–10), the diversity in language and variety in the human race is understood to be God's attempt to undermine the very human desire to use our clone-like uniformity to build a master race to usurp his sovereignty. Now exactly the same phenomenon in the New Testament is understood as the sign of a much richer and deeper unity as the gift of languages means that the body of the disciples, a group of largely uncultured Jewish fishermen, is given access to the whole world community. It is unity, not uniformity, that is the divine gift.

This is like the difference between racism or tribalism in our world, where anything different is seen as a threat and anyone different as an enemy to be expelled, and the perception that it is our differences, provided we have learnt to cope with them creatively, that give us the range of gifts and skills we need to make a success of living together in our world. Every now and then there is a series on television where competing groups are marooned on islands or put into teams to cope with some endurance test: those who succeed are always those who have learnt to use each other's skills and respect their diversity.

That is the kind of transformation that takes place in the early chapters of the Acts of the Apostles, and Luke is interested in this visible outworking of transformation, both personal and corporate, as Chapter 8 explores further.

Transformation in the wider arena

Transformation takes place very often as a result of the kind of face-to-face engagement that brings recognition. One of the ways of describing what was going on for the disciples at Emmaus would be that the breaking of the bread was the moment when the penny dropped – or when they tumbled to it? Both of these English expressions have a notion of free-fall through a seriously held attention into a letting go. One of the things that is necessary if you are to give your whole attention to someone else is to let go of those tight defences you usually protect yourself with, so that you can meet genuinely, face to face. So if God is to get a chance of transforming us, we have to be drawn into a pattern of encounter and engagement where our defences are down and we are less concerned with keeping our story and God's story in separate boxes. The prime example of transformation in our own culture is what happens when people fall in love, when the spark suddenly jumps across the gap. It is when a couple who have interests in common and may have known each other for some time sense mutually that their lives are locked together in a way that they hadn't expected. The sense of being a well-guarded individual who is quite self-sufficient is suddenly challenged by a glimpse of mutuality.

Another area in which this takes place – more obviously akin to scales falling from our eyes – is that intellectual recognition or understanding that takes place in the classroom situation. When people tumble to it, they say, 'Oh, I *see*'. These moments offer what Bishop Ian Ramsey used to call 'disclosure situations', when people caught a glimpse of how Jesus' exposition related to the overarching desire to build and reveal God's kingdom. The moment suddenly disclosed a deeper significance and became a small, almost sacramental, sign of the underlying reality that was there to be picked up. Jesus sometimes hinted at this happening when he said, 'He that has ears to hear . . .'

At the parish and local level – and it is true of many small groups – there are moments of transformation when you suddenly discover that the methods of working or the structures on which you relied aren't needed any longer. You can bypass all that because you trust other people to deliver insight and change. The building up of relationship need not be expressed only in terms of people falling in love; it is also visible in the moment when people are ready to trust one another rather than have to keep everything under their own defined direction.

We live in a society that is less and less inclined to trust the institutional expression of those relationships. We may trust individual people we know – the community police officer – to do their job properly, but do we trust 'the Police' or 'the Government' or even 'the Church' in the same way? We do of course need a system of making individual people answerable for their responsibilities, yet nothing creative can happen if controls are too tight. That is where the current debate about the MMR vaccine is so interesting. People would rather make their own decision based on their own highly limited medical knowledge rather than trust what any expert doctor or the government's Director of Public Health says. Why? Because they do not trust people they do not know, or those whom they suspect are spokespeople for a corporate view which may ride roughshod over the needs of particular individuals; they only trust themselves and their own knowledge. This is a sign of too great a distance between the government's chief health person and people sitting in their homes, of the lack of trust when there is no personal encounter. No amount of television beaming into our homes with serious and anxious and concerned doctors explaining the medical details will do, because those doctors aren't ours: we don't know them. People know perfectly well that where government is concerned, many things are put out as mass propaganda and that this is no guarantee of truth. These days people will not fall for that: we have all seen *Yes Minister*.

Examples of transformation

What sort of sense does this idea of transformation make in the wider world today? Let us start by considering some situations in which transformation is desperately needed. Then we need to look at how this might be achieved in a realistic way. So I am not saying that there is never a need for military force, or for undercover police work: these things may well be needed to protect people in dangerous situations. What I am suggesting is that we look at how, in the longer term, situations might be able to be unlocked.

The prime condition is that people meet face to face; if they do, and are prepared to listen to each other, then eventually they will hear each other's stories through the teller's eyes and learn to put themselves in each other's shoes. Sharing each other's stories is a necessary preliminary if they are ever to be brought together. Common to all those experiences of transformation are close engagement, person to person; person-sized communities, long and patient sharing of experience, reflecting on it, digging back into the origins, discovering where your differences in language lie in order to be able not simply to trust one another but to trust that the experiences you are describing are the same.

This process of engagement and transformation only works of course if both parties are committed to doing it, and are ready to put some energy into it. It requires everybody to be using the same tools in order to make a step forward that is recognizable by others. And it requires time and patience: trust is not built in a day.

That is why understanding this as a quasi-sacramental process is important and essentially as something God-given, because if this is how God operates and we are picking that up and working with the grain of his way of operating, then we can expect it to deliver the goods. It is not in that sense a human construct, invented by us, but a gift which reinforces, echoes and proclaims the heart of our faith. It is very like sacraments in the sense that this pattern of engagement and transformation is both expressive and performative. Sacraments proclaim and express something that is true about God's dealing with us; in the Eucharist he feeds us with the bread of heaven, the body of Christ. But they are also performative – they make something happen; in the Eucharist we are actually being formed into the body of Christ, not just thinking about it having happened once, but experiencing it happening to us now.

Christians and Muslims

A remarkable example of the quasi-sacramental kind of encounter I am thinking of occurred on a damp and misty Sunday evening one February in Salisbury. I was in a cassock and was just slipping in at the end of Evensong to return the cope I'd borrowed, when I met a tall, robed and turbaned figure at the cloister door. Eyeing each other, we exchanged greetings and fell into conversation. He turned out to be the Chief Mufti of the Sufis, here on a visit from Canada, and mesmerized by the building. We had perhaps only half an hour's conversation, ranging from the influence of Plato and Aristotle on our two faiths to the spirituality of place, and how physical space absorbed and promoted prayer, and I don't suppose we shall ever meet again. But I learnt an immense amount from my brief, fog-bound encounter with that cultured and educated spiritual leader, and came away with my attitudes to Islam quite changed.

Christians and Sikhs

An encounter of a different kind took place when I was a curate in Leeds. At the church primary school in the parish there was a large number of Sikh children, whose parents were keen that they should learn about the religion of their adopted country. They were very hospitable, and on their founder Guru Nanak's birthday we were invited to join the whole Sikh community, sitting on the floor of Leeds Town Hall among the marble columns and eating silver sweets. But they also knew that Christmas Day was the birthday of our founder, so that morning whole families of turbaned figures turned up for the Parish Communion, gazing with wonder at the processions. Our churchwardens were rather nonplussed, but we certainly learnt a good deal about hospitality, and the essential generosity of Sikhism.

War on terrorism

On a different scale, it is worthwhile too reflecting on transformation in the wake of events following 11 September 2001. While it was natural for the USA to feel outraged at what it regarded as an entirely unprovoked attack, and our natural reaction to that kind of massive affront is to lash out, is it right to seek a solution by military force? One side with every conceivable military power in its hands bombing an elusive enemy – not even a country – is bound in the end to fuel resentment and increase terror, and obscure attempts to discover the causes of that (to us) inexplicable hatred. Or, do you believe that in the end the world is too small a place, and that you have to discover what is common both in your humanity and your theology, and find out why the terrorists felt impelled to attack?

One of the major changes of the last 50 years is in the nature of warfare. At the time of the First and even Second World Wars, military action was about using troops, warships and planes to gain control of territory or access to supplies. It was almost like a board game, and the operations rooms of the period look just like that. Success could be measured by territory or sea routes secured, and conventions like the formal processes of declaring war, surrender and the Geneva Convention for the treatment of prisoners were all part of the agreed rules of the game.

But since Northern Ireland – at any rate in British experience – moved us into terrorism and guerrilla warfare, that whole landscape has vanished. No one knows what it means to win a war, because countries' borders are readily permeable and organizations easily infiltrated by agents, and there are no rules now by which you can judge whether you are winning or losing. And because so little is visible, there is no way of assessing whether protocols like the Geneva Convention on prisoners are being observed. Nobody knows if those who are being held are prisoners or terrorists: we have no mechanism for deciding.

In this foggy landscape, the brightest hope seems to be in those groups and agencies that keep contacts alive and conversation going. We may not feel that it is very effective – and clearly the

United States thinks it has the right to usurp that role when it wants to – but the United Nations is all that we have on the international front to which the nations of the world are ready to assent.

Brokering across boundaries

Here are three examples of brokering across boundaries, one from the world of conversations between churches, one from the world of community initiatives in peacemaking and one from what can be achieved by professional brokering. What transforms the situation is not just that people begin to form relationships as they talk across their differences, but that people discover they are talking about the same thing and want the same. That is the model that one would like to see for international diplomacy and which holds out the only hope we have in many situations. There is only one way to achieve it, and that is to sit and talk, however long and painful the process may be.

1 The Anglican–Roman Catholic International Commission (ARCIC)

Divisions and disagreements between Christians have divided the Church from early times. The divisions are frequently over deeply held matters of tradition, faith and interpretation, and are exacerbated by the fact that we use different languages with their inherently different conceptual frameworks. There are many areas of relationships between the churches where transformation is needed, but the Anglican–Roman Catholic International Commission is one example where talks over a long period seem to have genuinely changed the situation and brought people together after some 400 years of division. What was so different about the way ARCIC did it? Because the conversations ran over a long period, and over 10, 15 or 20 years the group got to know and to trust each other, and came to understand what the other was saying. As they began to enter one another's history and language, people on the Roman side began to understand what the language of the Reformation was about, and the Anglicans began to understand how the Romans were now stepping beyond their Thomist philosophical framework on which the Reformation had focused its attacks. As a result of going back to study the Bible together, of experiencing being Church together, of living, eating and worshipping together, the participants began to find that they had a common mind even if traditionally their churches had expressed things differently. This close engagement is what provided the breakthrough and brought about the conditions where transformation was a possibility. It is not easy to bring other people in both churches into that process so that they too share the same sense of common discovery that we might actually be talking about the same thing after all. The process of 'reception' by the wider bodies is no easy task.

2 Northern Ireland

Many years of bombing and violence by both sides did not achieve any change or transformation in what seemed an entirely intractable situation. But in recent years we have begun to see the same kind of processes of talking and recognition go on among the peoples in Northern Ireland. When they work together, in the wake of the Good Friday Agreement, on trying to provide, for example, good education for people, they discover they are after the same thing. That's the basis of the transformation. Key in the discovery of what those community values might be was the work of various women's groups, who some time before had spearheaded initiatives like mixed schools, believing that the cycle of mistrust and institutionalized hatred could only be tackled at a young age.

3 The Sant'Egidio Community

How do people get trained in peacemaking? The Sant'Egidio Community in Rome, a Christian but essentially lay community, has developed skills in listening and goes around the world doing it. They have acquired a reputation on an international level, and say that the reason they are effective is because they aren't anybody in particular; they are merely content to sit with people and listen to them and then draw other people in and sit and listen to them. The process of brokering is a process not of forcing an agenda, not of telling people how to do things, but of simply holding two sides together in the same space. It is their doing just this that brought peace to Mozambique, and they now have a worldwide ministry.

This pattern of engagement and transformation prefigured in Jesus

This pattern of holding two apparent opposites together so that the engagement results in transformation is not an invention of the twentieth or twenty-first century. When Jesus spoke of the temple being destroyed and raised again in three days, John's Gospel (John 2.18–22) understands Jesus to be referring to himself as the temple. The temple is essentially a precinct – a marked-out area like a football pitch within which the ball remains in play, or the district marked out by Romulus' ploughshare within which Roman law and order ruled, would be examples – where apparent polar opposites, in this case of humanity and divinity, are held together. In traditional Judaism, God was God and human beings were human beings, and the two were utterly and completely other. You could not even expect to get a glimpse of God and live. So in the temple where these apparent opposites were held together there hung a veil to keep the Holy of Holies where the Ark stood veiled from the sight even of the priests. In his claim to be the living temple, Jesus points to himself as the one in whom the apparent contradictions meet, the person who is both human *and* divine, the one who is so fully, completely and perfectly human that he is divine.

This understanding was revolutionary for Judaism, but it reveals how Jesus himself in his person actually embodied that quality of engagement that leads to transformation.

7 | Pentecost Changes the World: Handing Over Responsibility

The conclusion of the great Paschal cycle celebrating the death and resurrection of Christ is Pentecost. Pentecost celebrates the moment at which responsibility is handed over to the Church for continuing to live the risen life. Up to that moment the disciples had remained gathered in or around Jerusalem making only minor apostolic excursions into the surrounding countryside while waiting for God to do something. The Ascension signals the moment which became teased out in the farewell discourses in John's Gospel, that they were being prepared for life on their own.

But at Pentecost they discover that they are not on their own, that the Spirit of God is with them. The Church is being liberated to discover God's life-giving energy in all sorts of ways, and the change that they notice at once is that their sense of God's presence is no longer limited to the person of Jesus. The disciples can speak to all those assembled around them in their own languages and so the experience of God's presence funnelled into one person in one place and one time is put into reverse: God's Church, the body of Christ, is now equipped to go out and speak to everybody throughout the world, to each in their own language and over the whole of human history. The phenomenon of the Tower of Babel, when multiplicity of language was seen as a sign of confusion and dispersion, is now seen as a means of engagement and transformation with all peoples everywhere and at all times.

The Easter experience as a unity

In John's Gospel, the Ascension and Pentecost are brought within the frame of the Easter experience in a dramatic way. On the cross, Jesus forms the nuclear Church, handing his son to his mother and his mother to his son, and then 'giving over' his spirit as he dies. On the evening of the day of resurrection, Jesus stands among his disciples and breathes over them, saying explicitly, 'Receive the Holy Spirit.'

Jesus is alerting his disciples not merely to his resurrection but to the renewal of his relationship to the Father, saying to Mary Magdalene in the garden, 'Do not cling onto me, because I have not yet ascended to my Father. But go and tell my disciples that I am ascending to my Father and your Father, to your God and to my God' (John 20.17). John concludes Chapter 20 with encouragement to the disciples: these things are written 'that you may believe that Jesus is the Christ, the Son of God, and that believing you may have life in his name' (RSV). The Ascension and the giving of the Spirit are bound together with the resurrection and seen by John as a combined event which breathes life into the infant Church.

The early Church, in celebrating this one great event of the Pasch – death, resurrection, Ascension and Pentecost – over the period of a night to a morning, established the basic liturgical celebration. Later, under the more linear influence of the kind of thinking exemplified in Luke's Gospel, the unified celebration of the Pasch was teased out into its various constituent parts. This affected the Christian celebration of Holy Week profoundly, and has left us with historicized celebrations for each major event of Christ's passion. But it is equally significant for the way Eastertide is celebrated, including ascension within Eastertide and finishing with Pentecost – which is how we celebrate them now.

Stage 4 of the Emmaus journey

It is this Pentecost experience, and Pentecostal energy, that is reflected in the final stage of the Emmaus journey. The disciples have been encouraged to tell their story. They have had the prophecy of what God would accomplish in the promised Messiah set alongside their experience, and eventually have recognized that promised Messiah as the Jesus who breaks the bread before their eyes. Now energized – 'Did not our hearts burn within us as he talked with us on the way?' – they rise from the supper table and hurry back to Jerusalem without delay.

This is a journey with a specific purpose: the other disciples need to know that they have met with the risen Christ, and that he has made himself known to them in the breaking of the bread. In other words, the experience that enabled scattered fragments of a jigsaw to fall into place for the two at Emmaus is the key that all the rest of the disciples need in order to make sense of their experience of brokenness and loss and see the place that this pattern has in God's story.

Just as it was for the first disciples, making the connection between our experience of transformation and what God is doing is the key to sharing in his continuing life. And a burning passion to share his continuing life is at the heart of mission, just as it was for those disciples who ran straight back to Jerusalem.

Pentecost and mission

Discerning the hand of God in what is going on in the world is what we need to do in order to see how to contribute to working with the grain of what God is doing. How do we learn to look at the world and see what God is doing?

There are two ways of looking at the world. The first is the very black and white, death/resurrection way which says that the world is the haunt of the devil who walks to and fro seeking whom he may devour and that it is the task of the Church, as it is Jesus' will, to rescue people out of this sinful world in order to bring them safely to his heavenly kingdom. Alongside this dualistic world-view goes a model of the Church as the Ark of Salvation, sailing on the choppy seas of this world and providing an unsinkable refuge for those who can cling on to the lifebelts. The motto is: *Extra Ecclesiam, nulla salus* (Outside the Church there is no salvation).

But that is not the only model of the Church, and indeed a model which relies on very sharp boundaries with the world and on a well-defined and guarded point of entry may ring as few bells with people's experience as a sharp model of baptism which says 'one moment you are all darkness, the next you will be all light'. Is the world, God's world, so dangerous, so evil? Is baptism, or the moment of conversion, such a sharp dividing line in everyone's experience?

Most people acknowledge that after baptism it is possible to backslide and to fall into sin. It may not be long after you have been baptized with all the drama of the Easter Vigil, maybe only Easter Monday morning, that you find yourself cheerfully taking part in unkind gossip and tearing someone's reputation to shreds, or planning the deceptive spin you will put on your next press release when you get back to work. Unless you are seriously good at deceiving yourself, you realize that it is easy enough to fall from grace, and that the Christian life – however ardently we embrace it – is not absolute protection against the deeply ingrained habits of human sinfulness. This kind of thoughtless cruelty or bending the truth is something most of us do from time to time – and occasionally we find ourselves doing things which are a great deal worse.

Recovery from sin

This is why the Church developed a number of rites to help people back into the purity of their baptismal relationship with God in Christ. In doing this, the Church was able to point to the fact that central to Jesus' ministry was restoring the sinner, though even then his claim to do so scandalized people. Much the same is true today. People are not sure that the Church can forgive the sinner, particularly when certain kinds of sin are involved: no Home Secretary was prepared to contemplate the release of Myra Hindley, for example. But in a blame culture, even the concepts of sin and forgiveness are difficult. Is that because we Christians don't really think of ourselves any more as being in a state of grace from which we lapse? Today we are more likely to see ourselves as not radically different from everyone else – a mixture of our inherited genes and social conditioning, over which we have little control and for which we take only limited responsibility. In this kind of culture, the psychiatrist or analyst who deals with feelings of guilt by helping people understand who they are and why they are as they are is frequently the practitioner of first resort, rather than the confessor who is trained to tackle the spiritual roots of the dis-ease.

For the Christian, the whole apparatus of Confession and Absolution (as the Rites of Reconciliation came to be known as they developed into a complex transactional system in the life of the Church) together with the rites for Wholeness and Healing have evolved to cope with post-baptismal sin. The experience of Christians has been that however pure our intentions, and however driven we are by our basic desire to live for God, none the less in practice we don't get much of it right, much of the time. And you do not need to look any further than the Letters of Paul to the Corinthians to find examples of Christians sinning soon after baptism.

Learning to walk in God's way

But there is another way of looking at the world, which is much less dualistic, less polarized and black and white. It says that this earth is the context in which the struggle for the formation of human beings as free and responsive and loving is taking place. Human life is where we grow up by learning from the choices we make to take responsibility for forming our own souls and our eternal destiny. The earth is, if not a battle ground, then at least a playing field, where the forces of good and evil are in permanent session, and we are drawn into the game – a never-ending rehearsal over and over again – where we practise, as you might practise passing in football, or getting the notes under your fingers in a Beethoven sonata, to play the music of heaven. It takes a lot of practice to get it even remotely right, and the spiritual life is a constant patterning or rehearsing of the divine story, until it begins to become – we hope – our unself-conscious story too.

Learning to form and re-form in yourself patterns of personal discipleship and formation, and discovering that it is all right to get things wrong (since most of us learn more from getting things wrong than just getting it effortlessly right) and try again is how we are drawn closer to God's life in Jesus, and get our own into better shape. It is the spiritual equivalent of the gym, and provides a very different model of the Christian life from the transactional mechanisms of the confessional, practised to haul us back into a state of grace. In this understanding of how our spiritual lives develop, the practice of making your confession has more to do with letting God draw you into the pattern of life you long for and helping you step out of the 'sin that clings so closely', that habitual sense of wrong-doing that you are always despairingly trying to shed like a pair of dirty socks at the end of each day.

Until she was challenged to make her confession, Dora could not bring herself to receive the sacrament, but would sit at the back of the church with her head in her hands. Once she faced the challenge of taking responsibility for escaping from her disastrous relationship, she began to feel a sense of partnership with God, and the desire to change the pattern of her life.

Growing in the Christian life

Much of the growing in the Christian life that happens depends on this kind of rehearsal – a regime of gradual formation, constant repetition and gradual growth. In Latin, the verb *meditor*, from which our word 'meditation' comes, means exactly that: to pattern

yourself over and over again in God's ways. Letting God form the
divine life in you, in your community, in your church is the object
of the repetitive nature of daily prayer and the rhythms of the
regular observance of the Christian year. What we are seeking to do
in these liturgical ways is to build in those patterns so that when we
act, we do so instinctively in God's way, not ours. We do not go off
and look up what to do in a book of rules. Rather, by prayer and
study and the companionship of the saints on the way, we are gradually absorbed into the divine life. Our patterns of behaviour and
decision-making are already pre-rehearsed and shaped, and we can
step lightly – we hope – into engagement with God's world. This
patterning in prayer is the Christian equivalent of the Jewish tradition of feeding on the Law so that it becomes internalized:

> I have not turned aside from your judgements,
> for you have been my teacher.
> How sweet are your words on my tongue!
> They are sweeter than honey to my mouth.
> (Psalm 119.103–104)

Partners with God

In this way of thinking we do not see the world only as a place
of soul-making, an arena for our personal growth in goodness, but
also as a place that God has created and in which every creature's
flourishing and development is important and has something to
contribute to the harmony and well-being of the whole. We cannot
grow by ourselves as individuals without care and concern for the
conditions in which the rest of the human race lives, and whether
those conditions give them too a chance to reach their potential and
grow to perfection. Nor can we disregard our responsibility for the
natural order, for the care and conservation of our world and its
future.

 This way of looking at the world understands the Church's
mission to be about scanning the world and sharing fully in its life
in order to discern the signs of God's activity. What is God actually
doing in his world? Where are the signs of life and light? Where are
the creative happenings that look as though they had the ring of
truth or the spark of life about them? How do we discern which
they are? How do we help them grow to fruition and get people

mobilized to build on them? It is often in our hands to help seeds of God's transformation that could so easily be trampled underfoot or choked or clogged or remain starved of water, light or heat, to flourish and blossom in the wildernesses of mediocrity and self-serving.

The task of the Church

So the task of the Church may be understood not so much as rescuing people out of the world but as entering the world in order to share its life and discern God's will for it. We can then draw people together to celebrate God's initiative and help to bring about change and so take our part in establishing that kingdom for which we daily pray. This implies a less sharply dualist picture of the world. It fits more comfortably with a theology of baptism which talks about a new birth by water and the Spirit and which is interested in growth and development and the stages through which one goes in uncovering the divine spark that is at the heart of every person. It goes with the picture of human beings who are made in the image of God, where, even among all the dross that will need burning away in the crucible of love, some glints of the gold that reflect the divine glory are waiting to be uncovered. This is a different picture from that of human beings as inherently sinful, a state from which they can be rescued only by a radical death to self and rising to new life in Christ, which has often been understood as the only model of Christian life.

On my preferred model, discipleship leads Christians into a pattern of engagement with what God is doing. Discipling leads directly to mission – sharing in God's call to let his people grow up by engaging with what he is doing so that the process of change and transformation he has handed to his Church can be both continuous and seriously life-giving.

Mission: partnership with God at work in the world

We do not start from scratch, or alone, in this process of engaging with what God is doing. The signals of his presence are visible in some recognized staging posts on the way – experiences and even places where people have regularly gathered and lodged in one of the many mansions on the way to the Father. Where are the signs of presence? Where is good conquering evil? Where are people gathered together to create signs of hope and places of reconciliation?

The real question at the foundation of mission is about our understanding of God. Are we God's keepers? Does the Church own God in the sense that we can unlock the pages of the Bible or the doors of the Tabernacle and take him out with us, and see if he can do some good? Or is it more that God is alive and well in his world, and we need to unlock the tomb of the Church and help his people get out to lend a hand, so that what he is trying to bring about can be helped to happen? After all, this resembles what the disciples discovered the resurrection to be about when they went to the tomb and found it empty. 'He is not here; he is risen, and has gone before you', is the message to the astonished disciples. The risen Christ is out and about and doing things and wants people to go out and join him. So walking away from Jerusalem turns out to be not a slipping off home but a major reorientation, whether the disciples go to Emmaus or to the lakeside in Galilee. The experience of the resurrection pushes the disciples outwards, and forms the basis of the Church's apostolic mission.

We need congregations who are confident enough to walk out of church, expecting to find God at work in his world, and who can spot the signs of life and recognize that activity as God's. The Church's responsibility is to draw people together to celebrate this involvement in life, but then to move them out to help to create the conditions in which the seeds of God's creative life can grow and flourish.

Finding God's work

But where do they and we see the evidence of God's presence and work? Where are the signs of reconciliation between people and peoples? Where are the signs of the victory of good over evil in a gloomy newspaper-laden world where there seems to be an overwhelming preponderance of the victory of evil over good?

> **Recognizing what people are doing**
>
> In creating saints, the Church has had a traditional (and arguably cumbersome) mechanism for commemorating great and holy people as one way of pointing out the good news items of God's presence and work. A secular version, closer to the society in which we live, is the New Year's or Birthday Honours list where we can see who has been

given the OBE and for what. There are the stories of people who have
been pushing way beyond the bounds of what they might naturally do
for themselves and have succeeded in following a transforming vision.
Taking at random a group of MBEs in one Honours list, I noted people
who have contributed to the modernization of the Court Service, to
Oxfam, to the St John's Ambulance Brigade, to the improvement of
water quality, to the UK climate impacts programme, to the promotion
of diversity and equality in employment – as well as in the more obvious
fields such as services to education and the NHS.

What engages people in such sacrificial self-giving?

What is it that actually leads people to go beyond the conventional
utilitarian wisdom of what will benefit themselves, and help take
them beyond the horizons of their own limitations? What helps
people to jump over that natural fence of enlightened self-interest?
Sacramentally, that is what I was talking about when I referred to
the God-given spark, but in practical terms it is very often a call
from somebody – 'Have you seen what's happening?' 'Will you join
us in making it happen?' So the invitation to join the parent/teacher
association or to take part in a demonstration or to undertake a new
job in a 'missionary' enterprise, may be the way in which people are
drawn into following the spark of life.

How do you decide whether these things that look life-giving are
in fact the outworkings of the divine action or not? Is it anything
more than just backing all good, right-minded, liberal-thinking
people's natural assumption about what ought to be going on?
What are the tests as to whether this bit is seriously life-giving or
merely decorative?

Let me give some practical examples from the dilemmas that are
around in the Salisbury world. We don't want lorries thundering
through the city and threatening to knock people – and the ancient
buildings of which we are so proud – down, so let's get them round
the outside. That means ploughing a new road across the water
meadows, and we can't have that because they are an important site
for natural conservation, and anyway George Herbert walked
through them and Constable painted from them. So where is God's
will in that issue? It may be something more radical altogether, like
moving the industrial estate that is bringing in the heavy traffic
right out of Salisbury altogether.

Second, a parish priest in a sizeable village told me the other day that she was in a dilemma as to whether to support the closure of a factory – a closure that would bring environmental blessings. The NIMBY (not in my back yard) people who lived around, and made up a good proportion of her regular congregation, were very anxious that she should sign their petition and back them. And yet that factory, though threatening to pollute the world around it, provided jobs for some 300 people in the village, the bulk of the working population, and if it closed, the working community would lose its heartbeat. What is the right thing to do? That is the kind of dilemma that clergy are quite often faced with, where certainly one of the tasks is to broker some kind of resolution where both sides learn about each other's needs.

Then there are the questions of priority: should the Church encourage parents of children at the local church school to join the pressure group for a properly staffed crossing with flashing lights, without which sooner or later somebody will get killed? An individual may have to judge whether they should spend their time on that kind of activity rather than helping to run the pre-school playgroup for children, where they are actually dealing with the children's good in the here-and-now.

It is often helpful to try to see things from God's perspective as well as through the eyes of all concerned, and not only with our own immediate benefit in view, but also trying to perceive a larger picture against the background of eternity.

How do we recognize that it is God's work?
The world is a risky place, where there is a constant battle between the forces of light and darkness. But it's not all dark: there are great chinks of light out there, great moments when the natural goodness of the world and the supernatural goodness of people to one another are being revealed. There are bits of peace breaking out in spite of all appearances to the contrary. Remember the women of Northern Ireland who decided they had had enough of violence? Among the criteria by which we discern whether it's God that is at work, I list:

* some element of sacrificial transformation, drawing people beyond the normal limits of their horizons;
* some sense of unearned or unmerited 'gift'; it is not all generated by us;

- some element of breaking down the walls of division or achieving a reconciliation or new stage in a relationship (cf. Ephesians 2.11–22);
- some evidence of what Paul calls 'the gifts of the Spirit' (cf. Galatians 5.16–24);
- some sense of original creativity, whether imaginative, intellectual or artistic.

So what does the Christian do about it; is it simply a matter of recognizing what the issue or opportunity is, pointing it out and gathering others around it to celebrate it and therefore make it happen more readily? That certainly fits one of the sacramental principles: that the sacraments both reveal what God is doing, but also that by doing so they actually make it happen. But I would hope that the Church might be ready for a more proactive engagement.

A spiral of understanding

There is a useful tool that helps us, whether individually or working in a group, to see what is happening in our context and to evaluate and judge it in the light of our Christian understanding. We can then take action on the basis of our understanding.

This is a pattern of understanding and decision-making used by the Young Christian Workers:

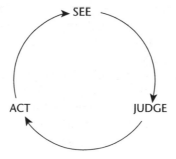

In this circle, or cycle, we first observe what is happening, then we judge and evaluate what we have seen, and then we take action. By taking action we find ourselves in a new place where we can see more than we could at the beginning, and so we are poised to begin the cycle again, seeing, judging and acting on the more developed basis. This gives the cycle more the feel of a spiral.

Other versions of this have developed and are used both in churches and in secular contexts where it is often called the Pastoral Cycle.

The rise of fascist politics

A good example, which is highly relevant to recent developments in many countries in Europe, would be events in the Isle of Dogs in the East End of London, following the election of a British National Party candidate to the local council in 1993. The parish priest in the Isle of Dogs at the time, Nick Holtam, wrote:

> On the following Sunday, the congregation at the Anglican parish church, Christ Church, were asked to write how they felt on a sheet of paper. 'Angry', 'Tearful', 'Ashamed', 'Frightened', 'Pissed off' were among the feelings. One elderly man, a member of the British Legion, left the church in tears. 'I spent four years of my life fighting Nazis, and now we've voted them in.' The congregation were also asked to write up their suggestions for what we could do. Dozens of ideas were put up. The Anglican ministers shared these with their ecumenical colleagues at our weekly prayers. We decided to call a meeting of people from all the churches to see if we could work on a constructive agenda.

A great deal of work was then done, in five areas:

1 Truth-telling (important because much of the support for the BNP was based on false information – people assumed that Bangladeshis got preferential treatment in every area of life, which was not the case).
2 Building bridges – finding ways for people from the two communities to meet and talk with each other.
3 Housing – because of the shortage of housing there was bitterness about how housing was let and allocated; the churches got all the main housing players including government ministers talking to each other, in order to develop a scheme for increasing local housing.
4 Strengthening the local democratic political parties which were felt to have colluded with racism in the run-up to the election. Achievements included getting all parties to provide translations of their election material, enabling the Bengali community to join in local political life.
5 Increasing the size of turn-out at the next election, so that the views of those who were not racist would not go by default.

At the subsequent election the BNP candidate was defeated, and no more BNP members have been elected since.

Pentecost and breaking down barriers

This example of the churches working with people of other religions and of none in the community to further the breaking down of barriers of tribal distrust, of inability to understand each other's languages, reflects in a direct and obvious way the Pentecostal work of God in our world. It reverses the language, tribal divisions and hatreds of the Tower of Babel and instead uses the diversity of languages to communicate shared hopes and longings.

Mission needs a broad definition so as not to become narrow or exclusive. We can define mission to include engaging people as co-workers for the God whose work they might recognize but whom they could not yet name. For Christians there is an important point in the process when they need to name the God who is being revealed if the connection between life and worship is to be real. If we divorce the two, then we lose our sense of partnership with God, and begin to think of his activity, whether in creation or redemption, as being simply in the past. On the other hand, when we are working with those of other faiths or of none, it is not always helpful for the churches to take credit for, or to attribute to God's work, what is being achieved: that often has a kind of 'con' feel about it – that the Church is taking credit for something that the community did together – even if we understand the mainspring as God's doing.

Looking for transformation

What we are looking for is not just moments when there is some kind of activity that we vaguely approve of, or which seems good, going on. What we are after is the moment where change or growth is taking place. Whether it is in situations or in people, we are looking for those transforming moments and helping them to happen, recognizing in the processes of engagement and transformation something that essentially reflects the divine nature. It is the *process* that is the key in our search for God.

Where do we look for the divine nature? It is revealed, says St Paul, in the face of Jesus Christ – the God who is revealed as the one who engages directly and personally (in incarnation) and changes or transforms our lives (in redemption). The key to the nature of God may turn out to be not a search for abstract qualities or some more concrete evidence of his presence that we can quantify or measure. We may rather discover God in the way in which creative change takes place, in the adverbs that describe the quality of relationships or activities rather than in the events or people themselves.

> **Intercession and what God is trying to do**
>
> As Michael Ramsey pointed out, the point of intercessory prayer is not 'to make petitions or indeed to utter words at all, but to *meet*, to *encounter*, to *be with* on behalf of or in relation to others'. Intercession is about us being there, engaging with people and holding them before God, and not about handing things over for God to transform. In intercession we are drawn into Jesus' union with his Father; by simply holding those we bring before him, we make the link between those for whom we pray and Jesus' work of self-offering. That is why there can be no dividing line for Christians between prayer and action: to be is to pray, and to pray is to be. *Orare est laborare* ('To pray is to work') is the monastic motto, but it could well be *Laborare est orare* ('Work is prayer').

How people engage with one another

The first stages in missionary enterprises, then, have to do with the quality of the way in which people engage with one another or engage with the tasks, rather than a kind of bland motivation – that if Christians are doing it, then it must be a Christian enterprise. If we look at the way some Christian orphanages were run in the past, we can see that being a Christian project does not necessarily mean that everything was done in a Christian way.

What is – or ought to be – distinctive is the quality of Christian relationships; not so much what we do or whom we engage with, but how we do it and how we relate. For example, we believe that marriage has less to do with the legal contract and the sharing of property and possessions, and is more about the quality rather than the structure of the relationship. It is the adverbs, not the substantives, that are significant. To take another example, there is a difference between playing the notes and making music. You can play all the notes absolutely accurately and in time, but it is the way they move from phrase to phrase and shape the piece that tells you whether the pianist or cellist actually loves the music or not.

And while we are not trying to prove how much we love God by the way we set about what we do, I believe that the quality of our engagement with God's world ought to be distinctive. That is not to say that those who have no Christian faith will offer engagement of a lesser quality, or – most irritatingly to them – that we tell them that they are really Christians without knowing it; but at least those who are motivated by the mainspring of sacrificial love ought to offer a distinctive example.

The world is our arena

One of the dangers of church life is that people get hauled out of the significant things they are doing that are making a difference to the world and making life worth living for people in order to work for the Church. Being consumed entirely by churchy things is always a great mistake. Church should liberate, not consume, all people's energies, so that they have time to take part in the housing association or the PTA or the local political scene or the choral society, or even spend some time with their families.

This can be a major trap when the Church badly needs clergy, and we see a likely candidate. Sometimes we think we have done well if we persuade people that they ought to be ordained when really they are rather good at something else. I remember a young man who was brilliant at looking after kidney patients, but who was made to feel that he should abandon that and become a stipendiary priest. And there was an older man who was training to be a non-stipendiary minister. He was in a hugely influential position as Director of Health Services for a large area, and was going to be exercising his ministry through that role. But somehow he got hooked on church, and persuaded himself that it was more important to become a stipendiary parish priest. If they happen to read this book, I want them to know that I am not saying they shouldn't have been ordained or that they aren't good clergy; I don't think that for a moment – my point is that too often we just assume that a clergy person is far more important in God's plan than a person who is doing a good and creative job in God's world.

Recognition and support

Another key thing about mission ought to be that the recognition and support of what God is bringing about should produce in itself a cell of life. A group of people who are drawn together in celebrating what God is doing and helping to make it happen also begins to model community. Is there something distinctively Christian about the way in which people work together to achieve a common goal that is due to the way they are bound together in prayer, for example? Ought people in the wider community to be able to look at the Church and see that kind of co-operation between people with their diversity of skills modelling how to build community?

I believe that there is something distinctive about the corporate experience of belonging to a living cell of the Church where Jesus' command to love our neighbour simply cannot be ignored. Experience of community like that means that we cannot continue to think of the Christian faith as a purely private and personal concern, with no social or political consequences. The Pentecostal transfer of responsibility to us that is reaffirmed in the closing stages of each Eucharist challenges each cell of the Church as well as each disciple whose heart burns within them to model the life of the Holy Trinity, that divine community of love.

There are times when we can explicitly celebrate the God-revealing quality of a community's life at the Eucharist. The test is whether that cell of people who are animated by the divine spark is bringing about radical transformation in a wider community's life or not. To share in the celebration of the Eucharist offered by a L'Arche Community and to experience the magnetic quality of that community's life is to understand something of the transforming mystery of the broken bread that makes our fragmentary lives whole. As George Herbert says in 'The banquet':

> But as pomanders and wood
>   Still are good,
> Yet being bruis'd are better sented:
> God, to show how farre his love
>   Could improve,
> Here, as broken, is presented.

It is frequently a vision of how the transformation of those whose lives are broken might become the heartbeat of a eucharistic community that inspires the founders of communities. St Francis had a vision of a broken Church; Jean Vanier of broken humanity. Both have grasped that the mystery of a broken life is set at the heart of the gospel, and is the seedbed of a transforming experience which is a sacrament of what God is doing.

People who have a vision of what the kingdom ought to be like and go and get on with making it happen will always draw others into doing it with them. Building or modelling the kingdom cannot be a solo crusade. Some picture or vision of how things ought to be is significant as the motive spring that draws Christians together into community where individuals can share a vision of what the kingdom might be like in reality. That is how for example St Francis, St Ignatius, Nicholas Ferrar of Little Gidding, George MacLeod of Iona and Mother Teresa all started their communities.

The Christian claim is that there is indeed a connection between the nature of God's kingdom and what he wants to happen, some connection between the vision people can glimpse and how we might begin to put it into place. That means working with the social, political and practical institutions in order to deliver some of those values that we hold dear.

8 | Becoming Disciples: The Shape of Our Lives

Pentecost was not just a stunning, one-off event: it started a process of discovery of how Christians were to live in this new age. Looking at the early chapters of Acts and Paul's letters gives us a vivid picture of these early discoveries and the controversies they provoked; it is worth reading the first few chapters of Acts and noting the issues that arose.

What Pentecost started

In Acts 1 we see the new disciples as witnesses to the resurrection of Jesus, praying and planning for their apostolic ministry as they appoint a successor to Judas to join them in carrying on the process of *engagement* and *transformation*. In Chapter 2 we read of their distinctive common life: teaching, fellowship and prayer were undergirded by daily attendance at the temple and breaking bread in their homes. The hallmarks of their life included signs and wonders, the ability to communicate with anyone, generosity and care for others, and most distinctively – that they shared everything they possessed. Already we see the author of Luke–Acts linking the ministry of Word and Sacrament with Christian lifestyle.

Preaching was clearly an important part of their witness, but it was the new disciples' distinctive manner of life which attracted attention and brought the crowds to listen to the sermons, which otherwise might have sunk without trace, like so many others. Speaking in foreign tongues (speaking to people in their own language), healing and challenging the established order seem to have been the factors which drew the crowds for the first three sermons (Acts 2—4).

Their concern for those in need continued to be shown in the appointment of deacons to complement the apostles' ministry, and in their good works and acts of charity (Acts 9). Then a more Pentecostal challenge faced them: did Gentiles have to adopt Jewish culture in order to be accepted as Christians? Did they have to be circumcised and obey Jewish food laws? Peter's dream in Chapter 10 is the sign of a Pentecostal breakthrough. People could be spoken to not only in their own languages but through their own cultures. The Church was beginning to learn that God was calling all sorts of people to his service and that the Church needed to accept those who were called, even if they were 'not like us', even if they were people that the Jews had been brought up to exclude.

But when we read the letters of Paul, we see that the picture of the early Church given in Acts is not the full story. The churches founded by Paul, in a Roman Empire which was rapidly becoming decadent and in which there was a growing spirit of 'anything goes', were generous in helping those in need, but they certainly did not have all things in common, or share everything they possessed; there were rich and poor, slaves and free. In the Corinthian church there were other problems equally familiar today, such as sexual immorality, party splits with Christians condemning other believers who put a different interpretation on their faith, and generally selfish behaviour that seems all too familiar.

This is not something which happened later, after an ideal early Church came to an end; Paul is writing his letters earlier than the writer of Acts, and probably as little as 20 years after the death of Jesus Christians were having affairs with each other, boasting that their 'party' in the Church had the true faith, and getting into cliques of the well-off to have luxurious dinners from which poorer people felt excluded: what's new then?

But in spite of the fact that it was, and is, a struggle, there grew up a recognizable pattern of discipleship:

- people were bringing their lives and their stories to the breaking of bread and the prayers;
- they were challenged by hearing the word of God in the preaching and the teaching;
- they were being transformed in the breaking of bread;
- they were being sent out in the world to heal, to break down barriers, to care for the needy, to tell others about the experience which was to change the world – the experience that new life was being found in the radical challenge of life coming through death: wholeness and healing through the broken bread.

The experience of becoming a disciple today

The pattern of coming into the life of Christian discipleship in the folk-memory of the Church is the pattern in the Gospels. A simple call from Jesus followed by an instant leaving of nets, and with no time even to say goodbye to family and friends, leads to a faithful following in the footsteps of the master. This is the pattern that is reinforced in the tradition of the Acts of the Apostles by the call and discipleship of Saul, who is struck blind on the road to Damascus, and after only days of fasting and penitence is received into the fellowship of the Church and baptized. For many generations this pattern of searching call and instant response has been held before Christians as the model for discipleship, and the main objective of evangelization. So when Christians sailed to parts of the New World, they took literally the command of Jesus in Matthew 28.19–20 to make disciples of all people and baptized the native converts in the name of the Father and of the Son and of the Holy Spirit. This sense of almost forcible engagement and discipling, with the baptismal rites celebrated at an early stage in the process, became the traditional and normative picture.

But discipling over recent years has come to be understood as a more deeply rooted and gradual process. A more considered reading of the Gospels shows us that there is a long process of learning and growth in discipleship for everyone, whether they make a sudden and dramatic start, or whether their relationship with Jesus has developed more gradually. The disciples spent some three years in Jesus' company, absorbing his teaching but often making mistakes about what discipleship really involved. Paul had much to learn from Ananias and from Barnabas and did not spring up a fully-fledged missionary overnight. It is now generally agreed, even by people who would have been thought to have been modelling their discipling on the more dramatic and sudden pattern of Paul's conversion as relayed in Acts, that coming to faith for adults takes on average four years.

The stages by which people reach a committed faith are numerous, and do not always follow the same order. For most people they are marked by at least some of the following:

- Engagement with the local Christian community which offers a welcome.
- A period of hospitality and shared experience of friendship and worship.
- A conscious learning of the elements of the faith.
- A decision to ask for baptism and preparation for the sacraments.
- Celebration of the sacraments of initiation, perhaps in stages, but culminating in the Eucharist.
- The working out of the implications for new-found faith for living life as a Christian disciple.

Patterns of discipling

These elements are those traditionally found in the catechumenate pattern of the early Church, and have been given prominence recently in the Rite for the Christian Initiation of Adults in the Roman Catholic Church. This pattern of discipling those who have come to faith has been explored and tested largely in the more sophisticated Western world, though it is found in the patterns of discipling in other parts of the world also. For those engaged in the process of sharing the faith and making disciples, a number of programmes have sprung up which provide a framework in which these processes can take place. The astonishingly popular Alpha course, originating from Holy Trinity, Brompton, has as its condensed basis both information about the Christian faith and a process through which people are guided from stage to stage in their understanding, designed to lead them to sign on as disciples. Perhaps the success of this course in a number of different churches, among those who are already baptized members of the Christian faith as well as among inquirers, indicates how important it is to link structure or shaping the life of discipleship with the transmission of the content of Christian faith, but especially the importance of hospitality and fellowship in the process. Not all programmes have both the elements of discipling and transmission of the content of faith, and the provision of 'formation' alongside the teaching of the elements of faith is clearly highly necessary. This equal partnership between teaching and formation is the basis of the important Emmaus course.

Formation

Formation is about the style of being a Christian, not just about understanding the faith intellectually. In the wake of the Reformation, emphasis on intellectual understanding was given a greater prominence than it had enjoyed, or deserves; hence the reluctance in some quarters to admit children to Communion 'until they can understand'. But is an adult's understanding, or a theologian's, necessarily nearer the truth?

Different models of formation suit different people's temperaments. Some people are naturally more at ease with a picture of themselves as explorers, as constant learners, as those who see the world as providing challenges and opportunities for growth and development day by day. Other people are more secure with a picture of a naughty world from which they have been delivered, a Church which is a secure ark, and a heaven which is theirs already. They are more concerned to know and have the assurance that by faith they already enjoy a relationship with Jesus from which nothing can tear them.

Both patterns have their roots in different aspects of the teachings of Jesus and of St Paul, and we can find support for both models in the Fathers and the liturgical traditions of the Church alike. So both are equally available to people.

What is important in the process of discipling for those who are taking part in this process and have already come to faith is that they themselves should recognize that they are accompanying others and not teaching them. It is not that they have all the answers and are handing them over to those who are asking the questions, but rather that together they are embarked upon an exploration of the meaning and purpose of the Christian faith in a particular context. That context is not merely the social, political and economic context of early twenty-first-century Britain but the particular context of sharing together in a local faith community with its own opportunities for expressing the faith, its own tradition of worship and its own pursuit of growth in understanding as a local church community while it seeks to become more mature. It is that sense of shared discipleship and being fellow pilgrims on the way that is most distinctively characteristic of the method and pattern that courses such as Emmaus offer.

Behind these patterns lies not only the pattern generally derived from Luke 24, but also a pattern grounded in our understanding of the stages through which human beings' experience develops. Social anthropologists have helped us to understand alongside the stages of child development the stages of bereavement and letting go that accompany the death of those we love. Most significantly for discipleship, they help us to understand the stages of learning and development that enable us to chart programmes for Christian formation with a reasonable hope of success. The liturgies that accompany the Rite for Christian Initiation of Adults are a case in point.

The Rite for Christian Initiation of Adults (RCIA)

The stages in the process of adult Christian initiation are carefully marked by a series of liturgical rites, ideally spread over a number of months, but certainly culminating in the Sundays of Lent and Baptism at the Easter Vigil. The stages include:

- Welcome, when the potential candidate makes himself or herself known, and signals a desire to belong in that church community.
- Enrolling for a period of conscious formation, including instruction in the faith, basic disciplines of prayer and a commitment to regular worship.
- The rite of Election, when the church says 'Yes' to the candidate's request to become a formal candidate and prepare for baptism. This is normally celebrated on or near the First Sunday in Lent and in the Roman Catholic Church may be presided over by the bishop.
- The Scrutinies and Exorcisms – brief rites of preparation celebrated on the Sundays in Lent, and culminating in the *traditio* or handing over of the *Symbolum Fidei* (the Creed) and the Lord's Prayer.
- Baptism, followed by Chrismation and Communion at the Vigil or Dawn Eucharist of Easter.
- Reflection on Baptism and its implications for the Christian life (the post-baptismal catechesis) and the making of a rule of life.
- Confirmation by the bishop, as a seal on what has taken place, a welcome into the lay apostolate of the catholic church and a commissioning for ministry.

What the Church is seeking to do here is to keep the staged rites of a number of Christian traditions in step with the natural processes of growth and development in the faith, just as the staged rites for farewell, handing over the departed, grieving, letting go and moving on are important in understanding the way in which funeral rites need to be shaped by an understanding of the processes that are actually taking place for the mourners. Both these processes reveal an important awareness of how the Church's mission relates to people's spiritual growth.

Once we can step behind using the abstract terms like mission and start talking about the way in which people catch the faith or are drawn or attracted to the person of Jesus, we can begin to plot the stages through which they go, and so help to provide both the right kind of welcome and embrace within the local church communities and models for their growth in faith. These stages through which people go are very close to those recognized as being marks of Cell Church.

Cell Church

Cell Church is not just another name for the home groups of a local parish church. In Cell Church each cell of the life of the Church contains within it all that the whole Church contains, and it manifests Church in a particular context at a local level. In the cell there are reckoned to be four stages – welcome, word, worship and witness. It is a programme for being Church that makes it easy to value and include people, help them to an encounter with the living Word, offer the opportunity for worship, and give people the confidence to go out and engage, putting what they've learnt into practice. Those stages are recognizably close to the four stages of Luke 24 where letting people tell their story, setting that story alongside what God has done, allowing for the moment of transformation and then doing something about it, are the hallmarks of the disciples' life. What Cell Church does is to provide a context in which the Emmaus pattern of Luke 24 can become the fundamental means of formation for the continuing exploration of the stages of personal discipleship in the Church's mission. As new members are woven in to the pattern, so each other person in the Cell is challenged and reinvigorated afresh.

Jesus' baptism in Mark's Gospel

The Christian understanding that new life comes through death was completely strange and alien to the world in which Christianity was first preached. The starkness of the way Mark's Gospel presents this suggests that it was written for those who could not cope with the idea; it seemed to them that Jesus' life had been a waste, a life so promising, but one which ended in untimely death and the defeat of that new vision he had promised.

So Mark's Gospel opens with the baptism of Jesus in the river Jordan, when the heavens are parted and the Holy Spirit descends, with a voice declaring 'You are my son, my beloved; with you I am well pleased' – a composite quotation from Psalm 2.7, a coronation psalm for a king, and Isaiah 42.1, one of the suffering servant songs of Second Isaiah with its connotation that the servant who will give his life for the people is the one chosen and anointed of God. So Jesus is revealed as both the anointed kingly Son of God and the one who will suffer on behalf of the people.

Later in the Gospel, Mark sets the story of the woman with an alabaster jar at the opening of the Passion narrative like a trailer, or prologue, to the whole event (Mark 14.1–9). There the alabaster jar is broken and the whole of the ointment poured out. 'What a waste', say the disciples; but Jesus rebukes them and says that her action points to the significance of his death. 'What she has done will be told in memory of her', he says, echoing the familiar words that so puzzled the disciples at the Last Supper.

Mark's Gospel ends with the veil of the temple torn in two as Jesus dies, the stone that had sealed the tomb rolled away, and the disciples running off, too frightened to say anything to anyone.

Yet the existence of the Gospel itself, and the community that preached it, was an extraordinary witness to the faith and courage of those whose fear had been turned into unstoppable boldness. In all this pattern of apparent disaster and brokenness, was there indeed some purpose or design?

The broken bread was the clue. When they broke the bread, the pieces fell into place and the waste of a promising life was seen to be a dramatic sign of the total self-giving of divine love. It was this upside-down movement from death into life that St John reflected on when he wrote, 'Unless a grain of wheat falls into the earth and dies, it remains alone; but if it dies, it bears a rich harvest' (John 12.24).

> In our lives too it is all right to be broken, like the body of Jesus on
> the cross, or the bread at the Eucharist; it is all right to be poured out,
> like the ointment for Jesus' burial, or the wine at the Eucharist. It is
> brokenness that leads to wholeness, death to life. This is the way of
> transformation.

How does our Baptism rite respond to our understanding of how we grow in discipleship?

The new Baptism rite in *Common Worship* takes the model of stages
in our Christian maturity seriously. Alongside the emphasis on
saying 'No' to darkness and 'Yes' to light (1 Peter 2.9), with the
sharpness of the cross as the badge of faith, and a clear centrality on
a moment of death and resurrection as the candidate is plunged
beneath the waters, dying to sin and being raised to new life in
Christ (as Paul says in Romans 6.3–11), it also embraces the model of
a new creation, as people grow into maturity from new birth by
water and the Spirit (John 3.1–5), and grow up on the foundation of
the apostles and prophets into a living temple, with Jesus Christ as
the cornerstone (Ephesians 2.19–22).

It is this model which fits most comfortably with what we know
of the developing stages of discipleship. In the early years of the
Church (as the post-baptismal teachings (catecheses) of Cyril of
Jerusalem make clear) the pattern of letting candidates experience
death and resurrection in the rites of the Easter Vigil was followed
by an unpacking of all that it implied in the days of the week after
Easter. Each day, the bishop met with the newly baptized and his
task was to say, 'Look back on your experience. You have been
welcomed into the fellowship of the believers; you too have decided
to follow Christ after coming to know him and learning something
about him, and you have embraced the elements of the Christian
faith. You have been grafted into Christ's life by your baptism into
his dying and rising; you have become members of his body, the
community of the Church. So what are you going to do about it?
How are you going to live as a Christian? You have been preparing
through Lent by practising saying no to sin, no to yourself, no to
self-will. The whole training has been to ally yourself with the Christ
who when praying to his Father in the Garden of Gethsemane was
able to say, "Abba, Father, not my will but yours be done." That is at
the heart of the Lord's Prayer which is one of the things you have
learned, so how are you actually going to do what is God's will and

not yours when you come, after these heady excitements of the celebration of the Great Week, to re-enter your life, your career, your domestic situation? What is it actually going to mean? How are you going to work it out in the practical decisions you make about how to live and act?'

Rule of life

Reflection on what God has given us is the mainspring of Christian discipleship in terms of how to live every day, and the Church is there to help people work out how they are going to shape their response to God's call, and then write down their 'rule of life'. Setting down something about your expectations of yourself does help to establish a framework, a considered response to what you believe about yourself when you are at your most consciously prayerful. Just setting it down helps you think through and then hold fast to some basic intentions about how, under God, you want to live your life. And you will not have to go away and work it out on your own; the Church accompanies you – or should – as you get to grips with these questions. We are all learning the way of Christ, and there is great strength to be gained from doing it together.

That is why in adult Confirmation classes, adult formation in discipleship and adult Baptism preparation, I would gladly give up a lot of the pre-baptismal sessions in exchange for a good number afterwards. It is afterwards that people find it hard. People get swept into keeping Lent and then celebrating Holy Week and the Easter Vigil with great gusto, but it is important that we do not just prepare people for the rites, but also help them work out how to apply all that the rites have meant now they come to review their life, their home, their relationships, their job or college or school – whatever it may mean.

What happens then? So often it is just at this moment that the whole sense of being part of the body of Christ, of having companions who have trodden the way before you who have themselves tried to work out how to live the Christian life, collapses in a heap and we leave people struggling on their own to do the best they can, with the help of some Sunday sermons which may well not be directed towards them, and the odd Lent course. That is where I think the Church's mission tends to be at its weakest, because it is often those who have become disciples recently who have the most energy for engagement. This is where courses like Emmaus are trying to fill the gap. The fact that they have such success indicates the great gap existing in the churches in accompanying people on the next step, which is to help people to develop a rule of life, a pattern of living in community, a framework of personal as well as general church support which will enable them to go forward in the Christian life and stick with what they have started on: faith-sharing by example and helping to build up the kingdom, not just spouting Scripture at people and getting them to come to church. As St Francis is quoted as saying: 'Go and preach the gospel; use words if you must.'

The hard work is in the interpretation and living out of the Christian life in a way that is really enmeshed in the current context of the lives we are trying to lead. That is where the sharp questions are being asked. The Church is hugely good at providing answers to questions that no one is actually asking, and not terribly good at listening to the ones they are. And if we don't listen, we won't engage, and if there's no engagement, then there'll be no gap for the spark of God's energy to leap across and set the world on fire.

The lifestyle of transformation

Does being a Christian make any difference to our lifestyle? Does the experience of transformation change our lifestyle in any way?

At the heart of the commitment to live a distinctively Christian lifestyle is a longing to live God's life, not ours, and the sense that the more we live ours, not his, the more self-centred, self-concerned, self-important we will become. In a world that does not trust other people either to deliver the truth or not to harm us, the dangers and temptations are to move back into ourselves. The security firms that control the private estates, the double locks on the doors, even the hedges of leylandia or privet around quite modest houses to prevent prying eyes, all are signs of people's desire for insulation from the outside world, which is what they believe will give them security and freedom.

Add to this the huge investment in insurance policies that build up the resources to insure yourself against disease and incapacity in old age (as well as to have enough to live on so as to be able to do exactly what you want without any reference to anyone else) and the picture of self-containment is complete. Counter to this runs the

Christian claim that you will only find yourself if you lose yourself, and that the way to life is through death, all of which is prefigured in the celebration of the sacrament of Baptism. But does this make sense?

A counter-cultural claim

Not in the modern world. Baptism is celebrating death to that self-contained, self-centred point of view, and this is immensely counter-cultural. God says, 'You fool', to the man who decides to pull down his barns and build bigger. 'You fool, this night your soul shall be required of you' (Luke 12.20). It is death that puts the question mark to even the greatest human achievement. What will you say at the end of your life about what you have done and who you have become? At what stage in our own personal development are we able to say to God with any kind of sincerity in our prayer, 'not my will, but yours be done'? This prayer is founded in the phrase in the Lord's Prayer, 'Your kingdom come, your will be done', and picked up in Jesus' agonized cry in the Garden of Gethsemane: 'Father, if it is possible, let this cup pass from me', and then his sigh, not so much of resignation as of quiet acceptance: 'But nevertheless, your will, not mine, be done.'

This serious pursuit of what God wants is at the root of a commitment to change lifestyle, and in a shrinking world it is as important for nations to be learning that as it is for individuals. A world economy cannot work when everybody is trying to get everything they can for themselves with no thought as to the radical imbalances that their own policies will create. What is relatively new in our experience is that real power is now wielded by big multinational corporations, accountable not to the public governments of states or nations – however elected or sustained – but to shadowy shareholders or unaccountable individuals.

So is it worth bothering? Most of us feel utterly powerless when confronted with the might of the big multinationals, and certainly governments do. But the Church has always been ready to stand on the side of the powerless and help the voiceless find a voice. We must never underestimate the power of a single act of commitment that embodies faith, hope and charity. It was one boy's picnic that gave the raw materials for the feeding of the five thousand. Where those virtues are visible, people will be drawn together.

What happens when I say all this to those whose lifestyle seems unthinkingly self-regarding, or who have the resources to buy their way into a better life for themselves, and especially their children? Can we expect people to change radically like that? One of the difficulties is that radical demands seem to be so very all-or-nothing: it is like the problems of Africa, which seem so cut and dried that there is no room for the shades of grey that seem to pervade every choice in England. How can we devise ways in our Western culture of getting some experience of being able to make choices for what we believe to be right by taking small steps together on a path when that can be marginalized either as a typical liberal 'cause' or as a fundamentalist ghetto?

Politically, it is interesting that we have a prime minister who is saying that working with African countries is not just a matter of pious altruism but a matter of enlightened self-interest. Here is a thoroughgoing Benthamite ethic of enlightened determinism before our eyes. If we do not arrange a fairer trade system with Africa and help them to find a place – even if it is a lowly or heavily circumscribed place – in the world economy, we know that Africa will not just be the breeding ground for a few terrorists, but that the continent will rise up on a massive scale. But where in this is a principled moral leadership that might win the respect of others, or help set a standard for our relationships on the international stage?

On a more local scale, how do we make choices in our local communities about how we will engage with one another? At the root of the attempt to help people to engage with the basic Christian ethic about being less self-centred we need to find practical ways of giving people the experience of change that is achievable.

Pastoral or prophetic?

When you ask a church about what it is doing locally, its models are very largely pastoral and personal. In our church lots of people help their neighbours: they steer the elderly across roads, drive the community bus to the hospital and are engaged in delivering meals on wheels. People will tell you any number of caring and pastoral activities that are being undertaken as church communities think about how to put the gospel into practice. But fewer of those communities are ready to ask the radical questions, or to engage in the more radical action which might actually change the system – so that there would be fewer people in need of meals on wheels, or fewer people living isolated in villages. It is at this point that the radical and prophetic models of being Church are much less attractive and much less part of our tradition than the pastoral and palliative ones.

Is that because as churchgoers we do not want to take responsibility for applying the prophetic to ourselves, but prefer to set our whole response to the demands of the gospel within a pastoral framework? And is this because the kind of engaging that would reflect the incarnate Christ coming among his people and asking the sharp questions is felt socially inappropriate – just too impolite? We know that in many of our parishes, where the prophetic challenge is held before people, they find very good reasons for disregarding it. In this diocese at any rate the style in which our Board for Church and Society operates has become consciously collaborative and reflective rather than challenging and confrontational. Such Boards are less concerned these days to champion the causes that no one is prepared to die for, and more concerned to help people think through where they see the signs of the kingdom emerging and how they might nurture the tender shoots.

Transformation by collaboration first, then challenge

To discover where signs of new life are emerging and seek to nurture them rather than challenge the grip of death by pitching in with radical opposition and proposals for radical change, is to opt for working with the grain rather than by confrontation. There is the radical challenge of the gospel, demanding that we stand the world's values on their head. But there is genuine theological divergence here about how you work most effectively and realistically for the kingdom. If you are being swept away down a river, try to use the current to reach the bank rather than use your energy in swimming directly against the flow. Nevertheless, there are times when only direct confrontation will clarify the issues and force a decision.

The patient work of one priest who has become chaplain to travellers in Salisbury is a case in point. Several years of just being there has paid off, not only because it has led to his being trusted by the travellers and showmen, but because the local authorities – especially the education and social services – know that the chaplain's insights are well founded. He is now a trusted friend and broker who can help the authority understand the travellers' needs and is well placed to challenge them when they fail in their responsibilities to that community which is so often misunderstood and so marginalized.

In the west of the diocese there is a creative partnership between the church and the school next door. It is a small school, and rather than build a new hall at huge expense, the school tentatively asked the church whether they might explore using the church building. The church said yes, and as a result the school has taken out the pews, re-floored the nave and is making the church a warm, well-lit place in which the children have their bodies as well as their minds and spirits trained. School and church each gave something to the other, rather than tried for what they could get out of each other, and this engagement has transformed the whole community.

And this kind of transformation by collaboration rather than by challenge has changed church life in other ways. I went to one church on the first Sunday they admitted the baptized to communion. Suddenly, there were some 90 children, from infants in arms to articulate ten-year-olds at the altar rail together, all looking as if they have a natural place there. This has actually radically transformed their understanding of what it is to be Church, and who belongs. Church was not just for those who are intellectually competent to answer the questions about what they understand to be going on in the Eucharist (as if anybody ever could); Church was the whole company of those who were included in the body of Christ in that place. Again, the process of nurturing children in the faith and bringing them to a point of conscious belonging rather than keeping them at a distance until they had passed what the adults regarded as a suitable intellectual challenge, shows the principle of transformation by engagement first at work in the heart of the Church's life.

9 | Following Our Calling: The Purpose of Our Lives

The headmaster of a monastic school was asked by some prospective parents what he thought was the school's aim. The headmaster thought for a moment, and then said, 'To prepare boys for their death.' The parents, so this apocryphal story goes, were somewhat disconcerted. But the head was surely right: it is death that raises the question mark over the purpose of our lives, and if we do not ask what we are here for, we shall never get a grip on the challenges and choices that confront us. It is in responding to those choices that we find we have shaped our destinies.

God's call: the message of an angel

When people come face to face with a challenging choice, they often become aware of a prod in a particular direction. In earlier times, people would describe this as an angel guiding them. Certainly, an angel often appears in the Bible when an unexpected message from God is delivered to a particular individual. Gideon and Joseph, Abraham and Mary are all described as having surprising news delivered by an angel (see p. 164).

But it is not only in the Bible; people on television programmes today talk about how they were in terrible difficulties or dilemmas and have suddenly become aware of a presence in the room (they often actually call this an angel) which gives them a message of hope or encouragement, or helps them to decide which way they should go. This is how it hits them. In other words, annunciations are taking place every day: this is how people describe encounters with a sense of the unseen that lead to transformation at hinge moments in their experience.

At Portsmouth Cathedral the clergy used to take the children's Crib Service on Christmas Eve in turn, and there was a certain amount of competition between us to produce something novel each year. I remember one year we did angels. We had prepared a lot of paper darts with messages and dressed some of the teenagers up in long white surplices with flapping sleeves. They climbed up into the organ loft and, unseen at first, began to aim these darts on the children below – initially just on one or two of them – and we got the two or three lucky children who picked them up to come and read them out. As they began to get the idea that these might be messages addressed to them personally, we were able to do a bit of teaching about how God speaks to us. Then when the whole congregation had grasped the idea, we showered them with darts so that everyone went home with one.

It's quite easy to write an important message, even for small children; all you need is 'God' then a pink heart and then 'you'. Most children who were at the age when they could read a bit found the message they received addressed directly to them.

Some of the later messages were in the form of questions, 'So what are you going to do about it?' It was possible just to take the children in the cathedral that day through a very quick summary of the Christian faith. 'God loves me; so what am I going to do about it? I'm going to love somebody else.' What we were doing was just starting the movement from thinking about themselves to thinking about someone else. That was quite enough. As they sang all those Christmas carols that put words into the angels' mouths, people were thinking about what the angels sang over Bethlehem and it was possible to make the connection between then and now. And anyhow, we had great fun. The teenagers enjoyed dressing up as angels with nice floppy-sleeved surplices and tinsel in their hair, aiming paper darts at people all over the nave; the clergy had fun interpreting for each child the message that they had got; and the parents of the children were made to think about the message of the angels now, and not just the fairy-tale stories of Christmas then.

God's call: knowing us by name

I came across an adult version of the same thing in Sant' Agnese in the Piazza Navona in Rome one warm summer's night. The Piazza Navona is one of the great gathering spaces in the world, full of tourists and teenagers, priests and street vendors, grannies and tiny children, all enjoying the fabulous fountains and ice cream, even at midnight. They had kept the church open too. There were five or six priests and nuns and an equal number of lay people counselling and answering enquiries as 200 or so – mostly young – people were drawn in through the open doors. The Blessed Sacrament was exposed on the altar, surrounded by banks of candles, and a music group was singing songs. There was the kind of rapt attention you often find only at the Watch on Maundy Thursday, and clearly a lot of heart-searching among the young. As we went out of the trance-like world, back into the crowded Piazza, each person was invited to pick a small rolled scroll from the basket we were offered. Each scroll held a biblical text, rather like the mottos from Christmas crackers. Mine was the opening verse of Isaiah 43, a favourite of mine, which we wove into the bishop's address to each candidate in the revised Confirmation rite:

> Thus says the Lord, 'Fear not, for I have redeemed you:
> I have called you by name, you are mine'. (RSV)

People are very moved by messages which they believe are addressed to them personally. This is one of the reasons for the success of horoscopes in the tabloids, or fortune cookies, or the I Ching. The sayings of the Book of Proverbs may be addressed to everyone, but if you took one saying and believed it was addressed specially to you, you would give it extra attention – an attention which it might well deserve anyway as part of a general collection of wisdom. But if it had your name on it – and that is why Isaiah 43.1 struck a chord: 'How did they know it was such a key text for me?' – then you would sit up.

In the Gospels we can see the effect produced when Jesus addresses individuals directly, indicating that he knows them personally. Rather unnervingly, he knows where they are coming from before they have a chance to tell their story. For example, there's Nathanael under the fig tree (John 1.47–49) or the Samaritan woman at the well (John 4.16–19). Most significantly, there's Jesus' encounter with Mary Magdalene in the garden, when he calls her by name – 'Mary' (John 20.16). Being known by name, known for who you are with all that that implies, is enormously powerful. If God addresses you directly and calls you by name like Samuel (1 Samuel 3.1–14) or shows that he has marked you out like Jeremiah (Jeremiah 1.4–8), then that sense of being seen through and known for who you are is inescapable. That is the experience of many of those who might hesitate to describe their work as 'a vocation', yet have the sense that they are doing what they are meant to be doing as well as their lives being personally fulfilling and worthwhile in the sense that this is what they have the gifts for.

Individual calling and our country's calling

Many regular worshippers work in challenging places – near here, I think for example of the chemical and biological warfare research unit at Porton Down, which is the most advanced unit in defensive research against chemical or biological warfare anywhere in the world, and may well have enormous significance for us all in the years ahead. Those in public and political life obviously carry heavy responsibilities at the best of times, and are under particular pressure when the peace of the world is threatened. But the behind-the-scenes work in places like Porton Down is where the sharp issues are being addressed, and I believe that as Church we should place such opportunities for engagement with the things that really matter at the forefront of our concerns. This is where Christian vocation is exercised every bit as significantly as in the more traditionally vocational fields like medicine and teaching. That is one of the reasons why we need a broader definition of the language of vocation.

This may also mean a radical overhaul of our priorities for mission. How much time and energy is it right to spend on maintaining the inherited patterns of the Church's life and ministry? And how much are we as members of the Church, when we look at our own individual calling, aware that as a nation we have a calling to carry out our vision of a just and caring society? And is it a sufficiently broad vision to enable us to see justice and caring as something more than working professionally in the obvious areas like schools, social work and the National Health Service? So that we see working at Porton Down as an essential part of our vocation to ensure the salvation of the world by protecting people in the event of that kind of uncontrollable warfare which threatens to engulf human life?

We all need to consider our own work, paid or unpaid, not just personally but from the point of view of the worldwide as well as national community. Where could you say that your work makes a difference? Is it in the growing or providing of food? Or of shelter? Or of security? Is it in the management and leadership of essential change? In the artistic activities which challenge the well-springs of human life, such as music or art or drama? Are you keeping the familiar going, or are you open to the new life and new ways that God may be asking you to explore?

The salt and light and yeast of the Gospel will never be popular where people are comfortable with their way of life, and where keeping the familiar going is valued more highly than responding to new opportunities for mission. But what is the Gospel asking for? How can we respond to the challenge?

I should ask myself these questions too: just because I am a bishop does not necessarily mean that I need not think about whether the work I do is worthwhile – in the Church, in the community around me, in the larger community of the world. If I look at what I spend time on, should I do more to encourage people to think about and manage change, and spend less time on helping to preserve and protect what people may like but which may be more of a comfort blanket? I have spent a lot of time on securing for the Church a liturgy that is theologically better tuned, linguistically more polished and more structured in its shape while allowing for a wide range of alternatives. It has been important to do that detailed theological and liturgical scrutiny properly, because it is in its liturgy that the Church of England expresses its doctrine. But it's how you *do* the worship that engages people with what God is calling them to be and changes lives. So doing the worship well and making the connections between what we do in church and how the world might be different are more important to me now than the provision of texts.

More fundamentally, how much of the basic administration and keeping people's expectations fuelled can I jettison, or will people give me permission to jettison, in order to do what I now believe I am called to do? What does Church need to be like in the future if it is to engage with how people actually are and offer them a vision of a changed life or a changed world which is actually achievable?

The calling of the Church

How does the Church as a whole ask itself these questions? There are some occasions, like a meeting with churchwardens, where it is certainly possible to move from the questions they raise about how to keep things going as they always have been to what their vision is for the Church tomorrow. Given half a chance, most churchwardens long to think ahead to what the Church is for, just as we need to think about what our lives are for. That question is more likely to be at the top of the agenda of the chaplains of colleges and universities, hospitals, schools and prisons who are used to those on the fringes of belief and at stages of critical change in their lives asking questions like that. At the heart of their ministry is how they can encourage people to explore the limits of their own integrity as human beings, and how that is constrained by or shaped by specific Christian reference or response.

But established patterns of being Church do not encourage each parish to ask the more detailed question of what is the vocation of that particular congregation, parish priest and parish.

Individual vocation and the calling of the Church

Vocation is a word that we are used to in the context of a parish exploring the possibility of raising up a local candidate for ordained ministry. We also meet it in schools, especially the secondary schools, where teenagers are confronted with life-choices and begin the process of matching up the gifts they are discovering they have with a career they think they might make for. And 'calling' is the language used when we explore the possibility of groups of farmers sitting around a table with representatives of MAFF and the supermarkets: it is recognized that the Church has a vocation to 'call' people together, and if they sense it's a serious call, they seem eager to respond.

Vocation is an important word for us, because a calling – 'a vocation' – is something that's not self-generated. Whether it is God who's doing the calling, or the Church, or the community, or even an awareness of our own gifts, a vocation – a calling – comes from beyond us and demands a response. It's not just something to do with ordination: it's what happens when any of us listens to God, or his voice breaks through into our subconscious.

When one of our clergy asked his 16-year-old daughter what she understood by 'vocation', he got the answer: 'A job you do for love rather than money', and 'Something you are called to do, not asked if you'd like to do.' And although we most frequently think of vocation in terms of personal call, I want to explore what it might mean for the community as a whole and for the Church, as well as for individual Christians.

First, the vocation of the community. Different dioceses provide different contexts and different challenges, but in the rural parts of the Diocese of Salisbury it was the foot and mouth crisis that changed how we felt about the countryside. We have realized how significant our contacts with the wider community are, and how valuable the huge contribution made by our Rural Officers is. Their work – both their personal pastoral ministry and their mobilization of a whole network of support and contacts – is so often under-valued by those who only think in parochial terms of keeping traditional church activity running.

The rural crisis made many people aware that we were in danger of spending too much of our time running church and too little in attending to what God was actually doing in the wider community. Where are the signs of life in your local community? What opportunities are there for creative engagement in what people find life-giving? What partnerships is the Church being called to make? I believe that the heart of our mission is to make new disciples, but that does not always mean getting people to come to church – at any rate at first. The risen Christ is calling us out of the tomb of the church to discover new life wherever people are gathered together. As the Church, we are called to discover the vocation of each community in which we are set, and help it respond to its calling. Belonging together in the life of the community is the first step towards discipleship.

Second, the vocation of the Church. The Church is called to be a community of service and sacrifice. We talk of the Church as the body of Christ, and believe that the quality of our life and relationships makes visible his presence among us. We put a lot of energy into the quality of the worship that is offered in our churches and into building up a collaborative responsibility for the Church's ministry. The exploration together of the gifts that God has given to each of us is equipping the Church for a confident ministry, and in this diocese many churches are on the way to growing their own priests. But questions about ministry have moved on from just talking about whether we have anyone who might be ordained. How is the Church to use the gifts of each person for what they are good at? How is Church to be life-giving, not draining? We are being called to discover the vocation of the Church, and equip it for ministry.

Third, the vocation of each one of us to become what God wants us to be. There is a continuing agenda for our own individual spiritual formation and growth. And there are some moments in each person's life when the question of who we are and what we should be doing comes to the surface. In the Christian community, we have a responsibility to discern in and for one another what are the gifts that God has given us, and to match these against what God needs done. This exploration of God's call is particularly visible at life-changing moments – choices about GCSEs or A-Levels, the choice of a marriage partner, the choice of a job, when the children leave home, or how to spend your energy when the apparent freedom of retirement beckons. We know how important these choices are: how should we be standing alongside people as they make them? There is a task of getting alongside teenagers in our secondary schools, for example; and those who come to inquire about marriage, or the baptism of their children – all these are moments when life-changes make it easier for people to be responsive to a sense of vocation. We are called to help everyone discover their God-given talents, and help them use their gifts to God's glory.

Expressing the vocation of the baptized

The concluding part of the Baptism and Confirmation rite, as well as the Ordination rites, is where this sense of helping each person discover his or her gifts and use them for God's glory is made visible in the sacramental life of the Church.

The Sending Out at the conclusion of the baptismal Eucharist is fuller. Instead of a Blessing and brief Dismissal, 'Go in peace to love and serve the Lord', the candidates are brought forward and given a lighted candle. The bishop reminds them that the light is not just a sign of what they have become but of their responsibility to live out the kind of life that engages and transforms:

> God has delivered us from the dominion of darkness
> and has given us a place with the saints in light.
>
> You have received the light of Christ:
> walk in this light all the days of your life.
> **Shine as a light in the world**
> **to the glory of God the Father.**
>
> Go in the light and peace of Christ.
> **Thanks be to God.**
>
> *(Common Worship)*

The baptismal vocation of each new Christian is to walk in the light of Christ in such a way as to make that light visible to those who are stumbling around in the darkness. The end of the Baptism Service in particular makes the mini-Pentecost of the Dismissal more visible. From the one Paschal candle small candles are lit for each one of the candidates: the tongues of fire that signalled the dispersion of God's indwelling life among the apostles on the first Pentecost. But with a share in God's Spirit goes a responsibility to use the gift that you have. Do not hoard it or wrap it in a napkin and bury it, like the servant who was afraid that he might lose it, but use it for God. 'No one lights a lamp and puts it under a tub, but on a lampstand, and it gives light to all who are in the house' (Matthew 5.15).

What is the gift that you ought to put on the lampstand – the particular skill that might give light to someone? It is worth asking people what they think their gifts are, just as it's worth my asking the teenagers I confirm – preferably with parents and godparents as witnesses – for a phone call on the eve of their eighteenth birthday to give me three good reasons why I should not ordain them. You cannot be sure that parish priests will raise the question of vocation to ordained ministry with young people who seem to have the gifts for it these days, and whatever we may say about the vocation of the Church as a whole or the vocation of each person to explore their gifts, the Church ought to face those who are considering what to do with their lives with the challenge of ordained ministry.

The vocation of the ordained

What the Church is doing in ordaining those it has chosen and formed is not merely authorizing them to do what the Church believes they are functionally competent to do; it is also saying that these ministers are being put on a public lampstand so as to hold before the Church something that is – or should be – generally true of the call of all the baptized. While we are all called to minister, not all are called to be public, representative ministers. Ordination makes visible in a particular person a distinctive call to the universal ministry of the Church. It is not primarily concerned with how that ministry is going to be exercised in the local context.

The three orders of ministry and our mission

Within this total ministry of the whole Church, each order high-lights a particular aspect of Christ's work, as Chapter 2 set out. Christ entrusts his Church with the ministry of reconciliation (1 Corinthians 5.18) and with continuing that work of our redemp-tion, giving us the Spirit to enable it to happen. The ordained ministry focuses the Church's mission in three ways. So just as the liturgy of the Church celebrates the whole work of Christ each time it is celebrated, yet we need Advent and Ash Wednesday, Christmas and Easter, Good Friday and Pentecost to sharpen our focus on dif-ferent aspects of what God has done for us in Christ, so the different orders hold before the whole Church different aspects of Christ's work to remind us and encourage us all to engage with continuing his work of salvation.

The distinction between these different foci held before us by each order are not always understood. I remember arriving at one parish church to ordain a deacon to the priesthood and being met at the door by the churchwardens. One of them said, clearly puzzled, 'It's very nice to have you with us, Bishop, but I'm not quite clear why you've come; didn't you ordain Andrew at the cathedral last year?'

Many people in the Church of England think that the three orders are bishops, vicars and curates (or sometimes bishops, minis-ters and readers!) with function and hierarchy as the basis of the dis-tinction between them, and services of induction or commissioning, not ordination, as the means of inaugurating their ministry. This assumption is understandable given the way in which various refer-ences in the Epistles approach ministry in terms of discerning gift and linking that to function.

Rooting our ministry in Christ's

In contrast to this more pragmatic approach, I believe that the place to start in examining the basis of a theology of order is with the work of Christ himself. As we said at the start, God in Christ does two things for his people: first, he shares our life, then he changes it. This is the heart of the faith, and it is the Church's task to involve God's people in the process of engagement and transformation and to ensure that this pattern is practised and handed on. This paradigm of the relationship between incarnation and redemption and the way this is handed on provides a model for teasing out the distinctive ministries of deacon, priest and bishop. The ordained ministry holds before the whole body of the Church what God has done for his people and gives shape to the way we use our gifts in his service.

The ministry of the deacon

The diaconate focuses God's direct and personal engagement with us: his sharing our nature in Christ's incarnation, his being rooted in the particularity of time and place. This rootedness opens the door to a ministry of attention, service, and the brokering that goes with the concept of Christ as the 'agent' of God. If Christ is the 'deacon of God', then the deacon is one who is commissioned to undertake a specific task or deliver a specific message, like an angel. At the root of this incarnational ministry are the twin categories of embassy and hospitality. The deacon needs to reach out into the forgotten corners of the parish to gather people in, and help the Church attend to the needs of the outsiders. But the deacon also has the job, and this is what is expressed liturgically in the Dismissal, of making sure that the whole Church moves out, and engages with the actual reality of the parish.

The ministry of the priest

The priesthood focuses what St Paul describes as 'the upward call of God in Christ', the reconciling, redemptive action of Christ's perfect self-offering on the cross. This sacrificial movement of response to a God who 'calls us out of darkness into his marvellous light' sets redemptive change at the core of the sacramental ministry of the priesthood. Movement and change are central to the paradigm of a missionary priesthood, but never at the expense of that unity with one another and with Christ expressed in the one sacrifice offered at the one altar.

The ministry of the bishop

Episcopal ministry embraces both diaconal and priestly ministry, but its distinctive focus of this apostolic and prophetic ministry is pastoral oversight. The mission of the 12, and of the 70, prefigures the distinctive Pentecostal mission of the Church. The nature of the apostolic ministry is to involve God's people in this process of engagement and transformation, and to make sure that this pattern is handed on. That is why episcopal ministry is focused liturgically in those occasions like Baptism, Ordination and the ratifying of initiation in Confirmation. Those are celebrations for baptized Christians who have realized that they are beginning to take adult responsibility for sharing in the Church's apostolic mission and ministry and its prophetic witness. It is here that the bishop's ministry as the focus of unity and the agent of communion with other parts of the Church is given expression in the ministry of pastoral oversight.

None of this implies that bishops are the only ministers engaged in the Pentecostal task: it is clearly shared with other ministers and with the whole priestly people of God. But it is the bishops' responsibility to see that the Church is Pentecostal and apostolic, engaged in holding together the diversity of gifts in a way that builds up the body in its witness to the world. Nor does it imply that this is all that the bishop does. The bishop is as much involved as anyone else in the processes of engagement and transformation. But it is the bishops' responsibility to see that the whole Church is involved in that process too, and to lead the Church out from the safety of the sheepfold to engage in its mission to everyone.

This sense of overlap is true of the other orders too. The diaconate is not an inferior order, where deacons never find themselves engaged in distinctively priestly or apostolic tasks: it is simply that deacons have *the* responsibility to remind the whole Church to engage with reality first, before attempting to transform – or more properly, to let God have the opportunity to transform – our lives. Diaconal ministry undergirds everything else, and priests – and bishops too – who move into a new sphere of work badly need to remember to start their new ministry in diaconal mode first. We need more deacons around in the Church who can hold this before us and help shape and co-ordinate the pastoral ministry of those many lay people who are ready to put their skills at the disposal of the Church.

The vocation to be a citizen

But there is a much wider frame of reference to this whole question of vocation: there is our vocation as citizens of our country and members of the society in which we live. We love to criticize our government, but our government is also our responsibility: we get the government we deserve. We elect them, and they are keen to be elected again, so they are influenced by what they think we want. Will they have the nerve to do what they believe to be right, and to challenge our pockets in pursuit of the vision of a more just society?

Much of the language of electioneering is not about the vision that a political party may have for our common life together as citizens of this world, where injustice and oppression continue unchecked in so many areas, or even as citizens of the countries of these islands. It is rather an appeal to what we want for ourselves; what will give us more money to spend on ourselves, better services – health care for us and education for our children – and fewer responsibilities beyond our shores for the rest. Election promises, even when they are not preying on our fears, are directed towards our basic self-centredness.

It is the Church's task to hold a vision of a different way of doing things before people. We believe that a vision of the common good and a sacrificial regard for the needs of others are essential to building a just society, and that it is the Church's *vocation* to hold these ideals before everyone.

The cost of our calling

Realism is vital. It's no good dreaming dreams or trying to respond to a vision of what God wants us to do without addressing seriously how we can turn that vision into reality. There is personal cost for many people in making a response to our calling, and we need to be realistic about this. There is also cost in the Church's response; it may be necessary to let go of some of the things we are clutching on to so tightly in order to move and change. Christian experience is that the things we had to let go of and sacrifice are often restored to us later in a new spurt of life and growth.

We know what we ought to do. But putting what we believe into practice is always going to be demanding, whether it's us or the Church or the government. We need the spirit of that famous quotation from John F. Kennedy's inaugural speech on his election as President of the USA: 'Ask not what your country can do for you – ask what you can do for your country.' That is the spirit of what I want to set before the Church today. At the heart of our life should be not what we want for ourselves, but what God calls us to become in response to his sacrificial love. 'Ask not what Christ's Church can do for you, but what you can do for Christ's kingdom.'

10 | Transforming Relationships: Celebrating the Sacraments

Piero della Francesca painted what is probably his most striking picture for the cemetery chapel outside Monterchi. It was to commemorate his mother's death, and Piero based the picture on the conventions of late medieval funerary memorials. Two angels grasp the heavy folds of the rich tent to draw them open. But instead of revealing the prostrate corpse of the departed, the drapes of death are drawn aside to reveal the strong, upright figure of a young woman who gazes out disdainfully. Almost African in features, she stands upright with one hand on her hip, while with the other she indicates the bursting buttons of her dress: she is not only very much alive, she is fully pregnant.

It is difficult to estimate the shock this picture must have produced by taking the conventions of the period and reinterpreting them so boldly. For the figure that stands there was not even the resurrected body of Piero's mother: the antithesis to this death is not resurrection but a new birth.

Like all the best artistic creations, the Madonna del Parto (the pregnant Madonna) takes our conventional expectations and transforms them in a way that both expresses something of what we long for and at the same time stretches our imagination. The result is a glimpse of a quite different order of things.

This is how the Church's sacraments function. They are the tried and tested celebrations of those moments when the Church has experienced a spark jumping between what God has done in Christ and the key experiences of our life story or faith journey. Sacraments connect the concrete details of our human story with the story of what God has been doing by significant ritual signs of transformation. At the heart of what sacraments celebrate is the making, reshaping and affirming of our relationships with God and with one another. That is why they are so central to Christian experience today, when we are conscious as perhaps never before of the vital role of relationships in our lives. How we relate to others, to our families and friends, our colleagues at work or with whom we spend our leisure moments, our neighbours next door or those who produce cheap food or clothing in countries the other side of the world, is the mainspring of our human identity. Relating this network of relationships to our understanding of God the Holy Trinity is central to our exploration of the Christian faith, and it is in sacramental celebrations that our relationship with God is both expressed and formed.

Sacraments are celebrated in a way that brings the community together. They rehearse a pattern into which people can enter and acknowledge that the encounter leads to a transforming moment – a moment when worshippers have come face to face with God, when their life has been caught up, even if only for a moment, and made new. In sacraments, this pattern of engagement and transformation is both expressive and performative. Sacraments both express and proclaim something that is true about God's dealing with us. For example, in the Eucharist God encounters us in the breaking of the bread and feeds us with the body of his Son, Christ our Lord: this expresses the fact that God does indeed give himself to us and feeds us. But sacraments are also performative – they make something happen; in the Eucharist we are actually being formed into the body of Christ by the experience of sharing in the celebration; we do not just think about that formation having happened at some time in the past, at Emmaus or in the Upper Room: it's really happening now in the celebration.

To get some sense of how the sacraments celebrate the transforming moments of life it is worth focusing on those moments in the human life cycle where relationships shift significantly. I have become more aware of this over these last ten years, when the Liturgical Commission has been consciously attending to the importance of celebrating staged rites to accompany those shifts.

Stages in the cycle of life

There are visible thresholds, when people face a new beginning in their development through the life cycle. Birth is the initial starting point, and birth in a Christian family brings with it the desire to include the new-born in the family of the Church, and to celebrate that spiritual birth with baptism. The British government's new proposals for formal Naming Ceremonies indicate the gap that is felt in a secular age for some kind of rite or ceremony that confers formal identity and acknowledges personhood.

As young people begin to make those life-shaping decisions like the choice of GCSEs, the choice of A-Levels, the choice of university, or form some vocational sense which may direct those choices and lead to the threshold of a career, they move over the threshold from childhood to adulthood. That conscious awareness that they can now take responsibility for making their own decisions allows adolescents to distance themselves from the person that their parents have shaped them into being. Stepping over this threshold into adulthood is often celebrated with a traditional rite of puberty. The rite of Confirmation has marked this stage as the Christian equivalent of the Jewish Bar Mitzvah, the rite of entry into the adult community and its responsibilities.

The next significant threshold may be that commitment to a permanent relationship with another person with the potential for the creation of a new family unit. Around the time of courtship, engagement, marriage and the creation of a family there are a number of stages through which people pass. Rites of engagement and betrothal traditionally mark the moment when they are ready to go public in the wider world with their personal commitment to one another. In some traditions this, rather than the marriage, has been the moment when a couple has been encouraged to begin adult sexual relationships, or at least go in for 'bundling', as sharing a bed was called in the early eighteenth century.

Today, we do not expect people to get serious over their relationships and commit themselves to life-long marriage vows until they have reached a certain age. We also hope that couples preparing to marry will have a range of education and experience which might equip them for making and sustaining those commitments. By having no formal rite of betrothal these days, do we fail to help couples acknowledge that this is a significant moment, when the quality of their relationship subtly alters?

Marriage and its consequences for the family

The next step has traditionally been formal marriage. Historically in the West, marriage was the moment when legal contracts were signed and the new domestic unit was formally established, securing both property and dynastic relationships in the case of wealthy families. In these more egalitarian days, although shared backgrounds and common aspirations have a strong part to play and may well limit the natural choice of partners, notions of romantic love play an overwhelming role, even though we know that without firm foundations of compatibility and complementarity in other areas, relationships are unlikely to survive very long. The Wedding Service, which celebrates this complex set of stages, often comes, chiefly for social and economic reasons, later in the development of the relationship than we might expect.

After marriage, the major lifestyle change for those who have married takes place at the first pregnancy. This is when the economic implications of the cosy family unit of husband and wife becoming three, and perhaps more, begin to dawn. Some traditions, like the Baptists in eighteenth-century Wales, have held that pregnancy is the key moment to signal the indissolubility of the relationship by celebrating the wedding, linking that with the birth and baptism of the first child. Is this the next stage in the marriage relationship or does the focus on the child mark the beginning of a new cycle of celebrations? In an age when the timing of the wedding is often driven more by economic considerations than by the relationship having developed to the right stage, and when almost 100 per cent foolproof contraception allows sexual relationships to take place without the likelihood of pregnancy resulting, the traditional sequence of these events varies more.

That is certainly not an argument for saying that before a child arrives all marriages should be regarded as trial relationships in which anything goes, but it may be an argument for reinvigorating the steps surrounding betrothal or engagement and marking that as a more distinctive stage of the process.

Traditionally there has been no other stage that is marked formally in the process of developing the relationship until children leave home, marry and celebrate the baptisms of their own children. And although a major shift takes place at retirement, the death of one of the partners is the next moment that is ritually celebrated. These days, however, there are likely to be various domestic developments, including when both partners take paid employment, and what patterns of home life and shared care of the children may emerge in that context. In addition, people nowadays expect to change their career at relatively frequent intervals as technological advances increase new job opportunities while closing down others, so the period between marriage and death is likely to be charted by a number of significant shifts which are not marked ritually by the Church.

Circles of relationships

In addition to family relationships, there are all the other circles of relationships through which people move. It is reckoned that most of us inhabit some six or seven of those circles – family, work, where and with whom you do your shopping, what leisure activities you are engaged in, what church or social community groups you belong to, for example. Those many, and overlapping, communities affect not only the adults in a family but the children too. Although many of those circles may cohere around the family home, a number will not. The experience of many parents, and especially the parents of teenagers, is that they spend their lives as an unpaid taxi service trying to ferry different members of the family to keep their different social, sporting and leisure activities as well as their scholastic ones in play, as their children develop their own friendships and circles of belonging.

Throughout our lifetimes almost the only constant is change; and relationships which remain static, or where the partners fail to develop in parallel, tend to run into difficulties. The original skills people acquired when they trained soon become outmoded and they need periods of retraining, readjustment, and quite often at least one change of career. So there may be several retirements and retrainings and new jobs during the course of a working life.

Retirement and rehearsing for death

These job changes and constant retrainings are all rehearsals for retirement and, ultimately, death. 'I should be glad of another death', says the narrator at the end of T. S. Eliot's *Journey of the Magi*, and with everyone living longer and the current cult of bodily health and fitness, as if this life was all there was to live for, there are certainly opportunities of practising for dying. Not that that's how many of us see it, in our attempt to outface mortality by amassing insurance policies and houses as well as investing in the stimulus of cars and holidays.

When retirement from paid employment comes, a person suddenly has no status, because he or she is no longer an economic unit, a wealth generator. In a society where people are valued more for what they do than who they are, this may bring a serious loss of

identity. Many tributes at funerals and memorial services recount –
often at great length – what people did, but the eulogists find it
much harder to paint a picture of who the person was. Yet this is
what we believe is most important. It is how a person has been
formed in the image and likeness of God that we think matters –
what will remain of the essential person, when the dust and dross of
their self-centredness is burnt away in the fire of God's all-consuming
love that appears to us as judgement.

So while I can sympathize with those who need to prolong the
farewells with memorial services and meetings, with endless tributes
and readings, Christians need good funerals that celebrate the union
in Christ of the living and the departed (which is why there is
nothing better to do at a funeral than celebrate the Eucharist),
rejoice that in baptism we have had a rehearsal for dying and rising,
and pray that the fire of God's redeeming love will leave something
of our personal identity intact.

In the face of a society that does not really believe in life after
death, and sees death as the final full stop, it is difficult to persuade
people that death is worth preparing for, and that dying well might
be an important part of life. That is where the daily rehearsals of
dying to self are important for Christians. They teach us that God,
not ourselves, is at the centre of the picture, and that what he wants,
not what we want, is what is ultimately important.

There is a considerable demand for sacramental, or quasi-
sacramental, celebrations to mark these stages of the life journey. A
number of them have attracted purely secular celebrations, like
engagement parties or retirement parties; and some, like Marriage or
Baptism, may be requested rather less than in the past. But in other
ways, such as leaving flowers at the roadside and in the development of memorial services, the demand seems to grow, and the
government is recognizing this in its secular equivalents like
Naming Ceremonies as well as Civil Marriages.

And new demands are emerging. The demand for a rite to bless a
gay relationship, for example, comes naturally from the desire for
people in same-sex unions to have a means of celebrating the commitment and expression of their love in such a way that will
continue to hold, form and shape the relationship as well as
express it.

How do the sacraments mark the changes in people's lives?

So what does the Church have to offer to help us express where we have got to and so mould, form and sustain who we are becoming as we pass through these stages in the journey of life? Is it just an aimless ramble, taking in as many pleasures and entertainments as possible, or is there a goal? Who are we becoming anyway?

Understanding the stages that people go through both in terms of natural social development – growing up, work change, job change, retirement and so on – is important for valuing each person and hearing their story, and for us to sense that we have a place in the order of things. We believe that we are becoming the person – or having the opportunity, at any rate, to become the person – God wants us to be. Our journey provides the opportunity for millions of encounters and transformations; the Church's ability to respond to the major and life-changing ones appropriately has led to an expectation that there will be rites to mark every conceivable occasion. Chief among them are those which mark birth, marriage, sickness and death; but there are also rites that mark the stages of coming to a mature faith, and of acknowledging the responsibility that results by undertaking training and authorization for a particular ministry.

The question that remains for the Church is how helpful to people are these rites as they make their journey? Which of them are absolutely essential? And most important of all, does celebrating a sacrament change anything?

The Western tradition has come to see some of these rites as sacramental, but not all. The rites of Baptism, of Confirmation, of Wholeness and Healing, and the rites of Reconciliation have belonged together in the bundle which affirms the worth and dignity of each person. These rites offer ways in which the original relationship with God that is both established and expressed in baptism can be restored in the face of either physical illness or the breakdown of relationship with other people, with the natural order, or with God. At the heart of these sacraments is the creation, or re-establishing, of a life-giving relationship with God.

Another group of sacraments is concerned with the reordering of relationships within society: Ordination and Marriage are the obvious examples. Confirmation too can claim to be primarily about reshaping the baptized person's relationship with the universal

Church through the bishop. This group of sacraments is about the relationship of individuals with a wider community.

The Marriage rite both creates a single unity – the 'one flesh' – out of two separate persons and expresses that the two who have married one another are now an independent unit in society, declaring that their life as a married couple is to be honoured by the whole community.

Ordination rites not only have an expressive function in declaring that the Church universal recognizes a particular person to be authorized by the local church – the diocese – to exercise a certain ministry in the name of Christ, and therefore to have a universal authority and not just a personal charism behind their ministry; ordination also has a performative function. It builds on the baptismal character of the candidate, alters the relationship to the rest of the church community, and consequently reshapes that deacon's, priest's or bishop's spiritual character.

Confirmation establishes a relationship with the bishop, signalling that the person confirmed not only acknowledges his or her baptismal status and recognizes the claim of God's call on their life, but is putting himself or herself and their gifts at the service of God.

In all these ways, the sacramental celebrations established in the life of the Church express or mark moments of human significance; they also create or reorder relationships which profoundly change people's lives and so shape the world.

How do we experience change in relation to the sacraments?

If you reflect on moments when you have been conscious of being drawn out of yourself into something greater, you may appreciate what happens as we stand on the threshold of those stages of significant transformation that the sacraments celebrate and help to bring about in the consciousness of the Church.

Moments like that include for me the experience, as a young child, of entering the choir of Gloucester Cathedral from the nave. It was the first time I had been to a cathedral, and we visited Gloucester on a winter's afternoon. The nave was massive and dark, with enormous heavy round columns, and some ancient black-clad vergers were huddled round a huge coke stove. It was pretty oppressive and vaguely sinister. But as we moved through the screen from the nave into the choir, I suddenly had the extraordinary experience of stepping into that tall, bright, double-height building, where shafts of the winter sun from the west caught the gilded bosses of the angels in the roof, and I became aware of the sense of oppression lifting. I can't have been more than four at the time. That sense of change is what has traditionally accompanied people's experience of Baptism. Certainly older candidates who have been baptized by having their heads held under the water and then raised up into the light get some of that experience of dramatic contrast.

A second layer of experience – less personal and more communal – is what those who go and join a congregation at worship and sit on the outskirts often discover. I once experienced this in a French abbey, and sat in the shadows, hoping not to be noticed but just to eavesdrop on the community at worship as a detached observer like many people do at cathedral evensong. Visiting the abbey at Fleury, I found myself drawn into the liturgical action not by anything that was said, but by the sense of inviting space. That experience was very much about feeling that there was a 'me-shaped' space there that I could step into, that the community was hospitable in how it included people in its offering of worship and about how much I felt at home there.

I know too that those who have sat in front of the often-reproduced icon of the Holy Trinity by Andrei Rublev have felt themselves drawn into the space by the way the three angelic figures sit around the table, leaving a space on the fourth side into which the worshipper feels drawn.

Those are physical ways in which people feel drawn into a community that seems to have a space for them. But it is possible to be drawn in emotionally too. On a diocesan clergy conference, it was three young priests who noticed that I was out of sorts with myself at the end of the conference Eucharist, and their sensible sympathy drew me into a quite different sense of eucharistic community. They were observing – though they did not know it at the time – the effects of my having had little time to grieve after my father's death four months before. We were in Winchester for that conference, back in the place where we had celebrated his requiem and burial, but this time with enough space to take on board how much I missed him, and that it was in the eucharistic action that the gap in my life could be filled emotionally and not just theologically. Like other Good Samaritans, they brought me to an inn and took care of me: they took me out to a good meal.

The same liminal experience is true of sacraments like Ordination. Although I remember my Ordination as a priest only hazily, I have a very vivid impression of my Ordination as a deacon at seven o'clock one bright December morning in the chapel of the Hostel of the Resurrection in Leeds. There was a curious community there, made up partly of family and friends, partly of the parishioners of the church where I was going to serve and partly of the Community of the Resurrection with whom I had spent the previous days on retreat. Vested as a deacon for the first time and preparing the altar – an early freestanding stone altar with a hanging pyx above it – I was at once conscious both of being the same person and yet being transferred into another identity. I was not denying the community of which I had been – and still was – a member, but I could not but acknowledge that I was moving into another community as well. The combination of the early hour, the sense of being vested – or invested? – with a new life, and the sense of radical disjunction with the old world of Oxford and entering the new world of the industrial North, was very strong. I was the same person in the core of my being, but roles and relationships were changing around me and making me someone different.

Now, presiding at Ordinations myself, I am aware of the same liminality in the lives of those who are being ordained. They are no less members of the Church or members of their own family, but they are being given a further identity – 'further clothed', as Paul puts it in 2 Corinthians 5.4 – which will mark them out as the servants of the people of God. While it may be the Ordination Prayer with the laying on of hands that makes them a deacon, it is – especially for those who are not very used to church services or to the niceties of theological language – the fact that, following the Gospel of the footwashing from John 13, the first thing that happens to them after the Ordination Prayer is that the bishop takes off his vestments, ties a towel around his waist and washes the candidates' feet that signals this new identity. For the candidates as well as for those who form the congregation, this is what expresses the decisive moment in their new pattern of relationships. That's what their ministry is to be about, and that's how they are to relate to people.

Experiences like these lead me to believe that we ought to be developing our celebration of the sacraments in a way that makes what was inherently true in them more visible, and brings to the surface what they declare in a way that people can understand. What is done in a sacramental celebration needs to resonate with people's actual experience; and I hope that our new rites are helping to make this happen.

The particularity of Baptism and its related rites

The sacrament of Baptism addresses our personal identity within a galactic frame. What does it mean to be me, to have some sense of personal identity in a universe of molecules charging around and banging into one another? Behind our quest for identity and meaning lies the experience of being utterly alone, our sense of loss of identity and of finding it again. That is why a significant text in the Confirmation rite is the bishop's address to the candidate (based on Isaiah 43.1): 'Tom, God has called you by name and has made you his own', before the prayer: 'Confirm, O Lord, your servant with your Holy Spirit.' That speaks of encounter and transformation in a very particular way at a human level, addressing the question of where an individual person belongs in the whole frame of the people of God, welded together by the activity of his Spirit.

The key experience that brings adults to Baptism is frequently the birth of a child. Taking responsibility for another human life and its development is a classic trigger – the sense of awe in seeing the child that we have brought into this world as part of a cosmic creation.

Dying to self

When people come to Baptism to celebrate the initial steps of their spiritual journey, the first thing they are given is their pilgrim's badge, the sign of the cross. The Church gives us an annual reminder of that each Ash Wednesday, when we are enrolled for Lent with the sign of the cross in ash. In the baptismal liturgy the sign of the cross is what we are given in response to a basic renunciation or turning away from the works of darkness, and turning towards the light of Christ. Taking up your cross is all that Jesus promised to those who follow him. When there is an opportunity for candidates to face the darkness at the west for their threefold renunciation of evil and then to turn to face the rising dawn to make the three affirmations of joining Christ's pilgrim way, then this sense of turning, which is at the core of what repentance means, becomes an even more significant experience.

In this movement there is also a turning away from self and self-centredness and from being locked into the limited and the small-minded towards the world that is filled with the light of Christ's presence. The early part of the baptismal rite provides the ritual accompaniment for that essential change of heart and mind which turning to Christ implies. 'Not my will, but yours be done', we pray with Christ to the Father; and the mark of the cross, which is the sign of death to self and our badge of triumph in the struggle against the forces of darkness, is engraved on the forehead.

> Another way to make clear that the baptized are turning away from darkness towards the light, is by the moment the celebrant chooses to mark and light the Paschal candle. There is a general rubric in the new Baptism rite that encourages the minister to light the candle just before they ask those questions. When I celebrate the Baptism rite, I prefer to mark the candle with the five nails before the three renunciations, and then light the candle at the point where I ask the candidates to turn to Christ. That is a way of dramatizing the essential movement of this first stage in the rite. To the candidates who are responding in faith to the Gospel, the vivid sign of the lighted candle marked with the nails confronts them with its demands.

Turning to Christ
Whether facing west towards the darkness or not, the three renunciations of darkness and the powers and forces of evil are complemented by three affirmations, where the three verbs are what is important: 'I turn; I submit; I come.' The candidate turns to Christ and that's a complete about-turn. The vision of the ascended yet wounded Christ brings them to their knees – they submit to Christ. But they are not left there gazing in wonder at some distant object of veneration; the Christ before whom they fall steps forward to raise them up and invites them to walk with him; for he is the way, the truth and the life. That reference to John 14 is an invitation to a journey from death to life in pursuit of the truth.

Death and resurrection
The second stage of the baptismal rites celebrates Christ's death and resurrection, and incorporates us into it. This is made real for the candidate who goes down into the water and is raised from it, or who has his or her head held below the surface: in the words of

St Paul (Romans 6.3–11), the candidate is entering with Christ into his death in order that he may be raised to new life in him. But baptism is also a wiping out of the past (a washing away of sin) and an entry into new life. Baptism promises a new birth by water and the Spirit (John 3.1–6) and the candidate is offered a foretaste of the new creation. The starting place on the Christian journey is both an instantaneous death to the old and resurrection to the new. Baptism's promise of a new start and a foretaste of the new creation has Jesus' baptism, not his death and resurrection, as its model.

Anointing

As Jesus rises up from the waters at his baptism, he is anointed by the Spirit. God has chosen him, called him up into a new life and has sent upon him the empowering blessing of his Spirit. This is what is picked up in the prayer that follows the water baptism in the *Common Worship* Baptism Service:

> May God who has received you by baptism into his church,
> pour upon you the riches of his grace,
> that within the company of Christ's pilgrim people
> you may daily be renewed by his anointing Spirit,
> and come to the inheritance of the saints in glory.

This is the point at which the newly baptized may be anointed with the oil of Chrism, to signify the outpouring of the Holy Spirit. Anointing was the means in the Old Testament by which God's choice of his king was declared, as when the prophet Samuel anointed David. This anointing with Chrism – the oil with which sovereigns are anointed at their coronation – incorporates the baptized into Christ's royal priestly people. They are God's viceroys, chosen to serve his people and care for his creation. Baptism into Christ's dying and rising by immersion in water is complemented by each candidate's 'coronation' by the outpouring of the Spirit, their anointing with the oil of Chrism. The two are as inseparable and indivisible as Ascension and Pentecost are from Good Friday and Easter.

Some people wonder whether the sacrament of Confirmation does anything more than repeating that incorporation in the royal, priestly people of God. That recapitulation of part of the Baptism rite, with the same gesture of laying on of hands and prayer, is used in the rites both of Reconciliation of a penitent and of Anointing the Sick. Both rites are restoring our baptismal status: reconciliation, confession of sin and restoration to communion with God brings in its wake restoration of communion with one's fellow human beings and one's relationship with the natural order. This deep communion brings that interior peace which ends the schizoid split life which sin brings. So the healing of relationships and the healing of the body are both related to Baptism. The ritual gesture, the laying on of hands with prayer, signals the same enfolding in the love of God, whether it confers reconciliation or healing.

What is significantly different in the case of Confirmation is the public affirmation of that conscious belonging in the ongoing life of the Church universal, symbolized in the relationship between the baptized person and the bishop, the minister of the Church universal. Baptism is highly personal, yet when you have tumbled to the fact you are baptized, then conscious discipleship in the succession of the apostles leads to embracing the responsibilities as well as the privileges of being a member of Christ's body. That is what the bishop's prayer and hand-laying delivers, and why Confirmation 'adds value' to Baptism.

A note on oil

The Church uses three oils.

The oil for anointing with the sign of the cross at Baptism enrols candidates into the whole process, limbering them up just as athletes were anointed with oil to make their limbs supple before they ran or wrestled. And if you are going to wrestle with the devil, he'll find it harder to get a grip on a slippery body!

Post-baptismal anointing is done with the oil of Chrism, the oil that signifies membership of the royal, priestly people of God. This is the oil used for anointing at a coronation to confer divine sovereignty and the responsibility and care for the whole of the created order that goes with it. At Baptism, candidates are anointed after rising from the waters; at Confirmation, before the bishop lays his hand on the candidate. *Common Worship* suggests anointing with a chi-rho sign to distinguish it from the sharp sign of the cross that confers the badge of the Christian faith as a defence against the powers of darkness. Chrism is also used at the Ordination of priests and bishops, and for the consecration of churches.

> The third oil – the oil for Anointing the Sick – has no place in the sacraments of Baptism and Confirmation. It is used regularly in the ministry of healing and not just at the sick-bed or at the point of death. In these liturgical celebrations of wholeness and healing it offers a powerful sacramental means of restoring a person to their baptismal wholeness.
>
> These three oils are blessed by the Bishop on Maundy Thursday in the presence of the clergy of the diocese, who can then take and use fresh oils as they celebrate the sacraments of Baptism, Reconciliation and Healing at Easter.

The sacrament of Reconciliation, as also the sacrament of Healing, are both related to Baptism; in liturgical books the rites are grouped together because Reconciliation and Healing are both about bringing the person back to that sense of having died to self in order to live for God that is at the heart of Baptism.

The sacrament of Wholeness and Healing, with which the penitential rites are closely associated, also has a laying on of hands and anointing as its sacramental expression. Those who come forward are receiving the same ritual gestures as at Confirmation. At Confirmation, the signing of the forehead is an embrace by the Holy Spirit, a mark of inclusion. It's about smoothing the oil of Chrism with the circular movement of the Greek chi-rho – the letters X and P that begin the word Χριστοσ, the anointed one – into that place where the sharp cross was engraved on the forehead as the baptismal badge. In the rites of Healing and Wholeness the anointing is a sign that God is yet again taking us out of ourselves and back to our essential baptismal dependence on him alone, challenging us to think about not what we want for ourselves, but about what he wants for us. That is the proper prayer in moments of extreme sickness, both for those who are sick and for those ministering to them, just as it is in those less urgent moments: 'Father, if it be possible, let this cup pass from me; but none the less, not my will but yours be done', as Jesus prayed in the Garden of Gethsemane.

Receiving God's healing touch in the sacrament of Healing or the absolute assurance of forgiveness by the formal absolution of our sins in the sacrament of Reconciliation makes that direct link with the ministry of Jesus in the Gospels that he entrusted to his followers. Jesus healed and forgave sins; the Church's sacraments continue this ministry, as the section *Recovery from sin* in Chapter 7 makes clear. The sick may not be healed instantaneously in the way we often want so badly, but they do receive that gift of peace which comes from knowing themselves to be enfolded in the divine love – which they so often experience being mediated through the hands of those who care for them. And that is just how the sacrament of Reconciliation works. Knowing that we are receiving that forgiveness which the risen Christ charged his apostles with ministering at the hands of one ordained as their successor is significant; so are the words '. . . forgive thee thine offences; and by his authority committed unto me, I absolve thee from all thy sins, in the name of the Father, and of the Son, and of the Holy Ghost' (Book of Common Prayer).

Talking to those who have been confirmed, it is clear that while they are caught up in the drama of the liturgy, they still remember most vividly the challenge of being addressed by name and anointed with 'that round Greek sign', as they become kings and queens – anointed as God's viceroys to care for his creation and serve his people – in the moment of Confirmation. And for someone who was very sick, the anointing came 'as a moment of release, when I could let go of all the effort to will myself better, and let God have a go at doing what he wanted for me'.

The Eucharist-related sacraments

Other sacraments focus more on a visible coming together of people and the restoring of what is broken in a more obviously corporate sense. The Eucharist is the fount of these, and closely allied to it is Marriage which celebrates making two individuals one. There are other parallels between the Marriage rite which celebrates the establishment of a new cell of the community's life, and the Eucharist, as is made clear when we celebrate a Nuptial Mass.

What is not always visible with its inevitable concentration on the two individuals concerned, is Marriage's communitarian and social significance. The new *Common Worship* Marriage Service has several pointers towards that. The couple are introduced and charged before prayer and a Liturgy of the Word, with questions being asked of the whole congregation about whether they will support the couple in their life together. After the exchange of vows and rings and the joining of hands, the couple receives one of the new nuptial blessings. These make it quite clear that the marriage is not just two individual people now getting legally joined, but the two of them are becoming one, as a sign and realization of the new creation. They are assigned a place in the wider community in which they will live their married life, not only so that they can be supported and upheld in it, but also so that their new cell of community can help in providing another example of togetherness in a world that is falling apart.

God's purpose is the building up and not breaking down of relationships, so that people find their fulfilment in relationship and not in isolation. That is another sacramental sign of the creation of community. In Marriage, the whole is much greater than the sum of the parts, and it is in that sense that transformation takes place: in these two people together there is not only the literal promise of a new creation in the birth of their children, there is an important sense in which both of them will be more themselves, more fulfilled, more whole people than they could be on their own. Otherwise, why bother with marriage?

The Church and Ordination

The other sacrament of this kind – Ordination – is about ordering the Church and giving it shape. The Church is the body of Christ, the people of God, the dwelling place of the Holy Spirit, and is built upon the foundations of the apostles and prophets, Jesus Christ himself being the chief cornerstone. The Church itself is a sacramental sign of the presence of Christ in the world. It does not contain him, but it provides a focus for the recognition of his presence; or, rather more simply, it makes him visible.

All baptized Christians, who have understood that that's what they are, are called to minister in Christ's name. But within that general responsibility the Church's ministerial life is shaped and ordered historically by the Ordination of deacons, priests and bishops. Orders in the Church are not primarily about functional responsibilities, though distinctive responsibilities for each order accrued as the Church's ministry developed. Orders are primarily significant for what they say about the way God shared our life in Christ, transformed it in his saving acts and then handed on to us the responsibility for continuing that pattern in the Church's life.

Deacons have a particular responsibility to make visible Christ's incarnation; their ministry is one of engagement, presence and attention as they model the servanthood of Christ, who in the words of Philippians 2.5–11 laid aside his dignity, assumed the form of a servant, and accepted death on the cross.

The Ordination of priests puts Christ's sacrificial self-giving on the cross at the focal point of the Church's life. Priests make 'the upward call of God in Christ Jesus' (Philippians 3.14, RSV) visible. Priests are ordained to provide at the heart of the Church an example of life lived in relationship to this sacrificial call, and build the community of disciples up into that continuing pattern of self-offering to the Father.

The ordination of bishops provides that Pentecostal sign of unity in diversity which is at the heart of the Church's lived experience. As a focus of unity, the bishop holds the different and complementary manifestations of Christian life together, each being valid interpretations of the tradition. The bishop presides at those occasions like Confirmation and Ordination where the apostolic tradition of believing and witnessing is being handed on: people are being welded into a pattern of life and faith, and encouraged to hand it on to others. This does not mean that bishops, priests or deacons are solely responsible for holding those things before the community: they hold them before the community to signal that the whole community has to take responsibility for them.

Celebrating change in relationships

All these sacraments are focused on transformation. Each celebrates a point of change, and in each case there are factors which bring people individually or corporately to the point where they long for change. For example:

- In the sacrament of Baptism, the divine spark in each human person is recognized and our dependence on God's grace acknowledged; that conscious relationship with God is created.
- In the sacrament of Confirmation, those who are searching for personal identity acknowledge their need to be valued; conscious of their own mortality, they embrace the new life in Christ through dying to self that was offered in Baptism.
- In the sacrament of Reconciliation or Confession, people long to be at one with those from whom they have been divided; restoring relationships that are fragmented is what people long for.

- In the sacrament of the Eucharist, people are faced with their sense of brokenness and loss of community; they are searching for a new identity, and the possibility of rediscovering that through being welded into the body of Christ.
- In the sacrament of Healing, people bring their broken bodies and battered spirits to receive the healing touch of Christ; they are longing to be made whole in body, mind and spirit.
- In the sacrament of Marriage, two people bring their longing to live a single, united life; they ask from their marriage an indissoluble seal that will help each of them to be more than they ever could be on their own.
- In the sacrament of Orders, the Church recognizes the gifts a person has to offer for the building up of the body of Christ; the candidate receives Christ's authority to minister in the Church, and finds their relationship with God and their community re-formed.

The three sacraments that are unambiguously dominical are Baptism, the Eucharist and the sacrament of Reconciliation. It is interesting that the sacrament of Reconciliation had become so privatized by the time of the Reformation, having become so much a weapon of priestly control, that the impeccable biblical credentials of its dominical institution were disregarded. But what is key about all the sacraments is that they provide formal celebrations that crystallize those moments when the Church recognizes God's transforming action at work. These are moments of God's transforming action, not ours, where there has been encounter to which we have responded and which draws the community of the Church together to celebrate, making us one with one another and one with God, making, transforming, energizing and re-establishing those relationships which are at the heart of our participation in the divine life.

The Church has always taught that the sacraments are effective signs which bring the ministry of Christ into conjunction with key moments of our lives. Healing, forgiveness, baptism, commissioning, marriage and Eucharist were part of Christ's ministry, instituted or blessed by Christ himself. The Church has always recognized in these sacraments a continuing disclosure of the activity of Christ in his Church, which is universally recognizable.

We should never forget the power of the sacramental celebration to challenge and convert, as Prince Vladimir's emissaries discovered.

Searching for an appropriate faith for his people, Prince Vladimir of Kiev is said to have sent ambassadors to a variety of countries to learn about their religion and worship in the year 987. They were not very impressed with the Muslim Bulgars, and among the Germans (Christians in the Western tradition), the ambassadors reported they saw 'no glory'. But in Constantinople they were taken to Hagia Sophia, the great church of the Holy Wisdom, and the report of what they experienced there convinced the Prince, whose subjects were baptized as Eastern Christians.

We knew not whether we were in heaven or on earth. For on earth there is no such splendour or such beauty, and we are at a loss how to describe it. We know only that God dwells there among men, and their service is fairer than the ceremonies of other nations. For we cannot forget that beauty.

11 | Celebrating Change in People's Lives: Sacramental Moments

The Church has traditionally defined sacraments in relation to Jesus' ministry. For example, Jesus' Baptism provides the model for our Baptism and initiation into a life lived consciously under God; the Gospels are full of healings, of the absolution and forgiveness of sins, and Jesus attended and graced a marriage. The commissioning of Jesus' disciples by washing their feet at the Last Supper and breathing over them behind the locked doors has a clear baptismal reference. But when these Johannine accounts are read as the Gospels at the Ordinations of deacons and priests, the newly ordained are being given a particular focus for their ministry in the succession of those first apostles. All these moments when Jesus' actions are disclosed as direct links between what he does and what the Father wills are typified in the Eucharist – the bread broken at the Last Supper, the body broken on the cross and the risen presence among his disciples as they broke bread.

The sacraments are the public celebrations of our relationship with Christ. Our celebration of them changes the nature of our relationship with him or develops it in some way. Baptism and its subsidiary, Confirmation, initiates, and then makes public, the relationship. The Eucharist nourishes it and sustains it. The sacraments of Reconciliation and Healing restore the relationship. Marriage gives us a worked example of the relationship; and Ordination establishes a pattern of relationships within the Church's ministry that makes Christ's ministry visible.

The whole of life as sacramental

As well as the public sacraments, the Church has many other ritual acts which have their origin in marking everyday events, objects and places as sacramental and so helping to link our story with Christ's transforming life. They are not the sacraments, instituted by Christ and acknowledged by the whole of the Church as performative signs that change or establish relationships. They are markers in seeing the whole of life as sacramental, in other words in offering us opportunities for recognizing the world and what goes on in it as a means of encountering and recognizing God. Sometimes known as sacramentals, these markers are often connected with moments of recollection and informal prayer, and include such things as making the sign of the cross, foot washing and saying grace at meals, or with other blessings, like the blessing of a house or a new ship, or with objects like a crucifix or an icon.

Sacramentals

Foot washing, for example, is something instituted by Christ himself as an illustrative sign for his disciples (John 13). This inclusive sign inaugurated what the Church came to formalize as diaconal ministry, just as breathing on the disciples gathered behind the closed doors (John 20) signalled the inauguration of the ministry of reconciliation. This is the ministry of the new creation, inaugurated by water and the Spirit (John 3). Another teaching episode in the Gospels shows Jesus taking a child, setting him up in front of his disciples who had been arguing about who was the greatest, and telling them that if any would be first, they must be last of all and servant of all (Mark 9.33–37). This is the origin of the medieval Christmastide tradition in many cathedrals of the Boy Bishop, where the bishop changed places with a young chorister during the verses of the Magnificat at Vespers that say:

> He has put down the mighty from their seat,
> and has exalted the humble and meek.

and the chorister then acted as bishop for a time. Other sacramentals, such as saying grace before meals, or childhood prayers for protection at going to bed –

> Matthew, Mark, Luke and John
> bless the bed that I lie on –

relate more closely to the Jewish tradition of the head of the household blessing God for his gifts in a variety of ways. In the Hebrew prayer book there are a number of blessings, such as this one, said on tasting any fruit for the first time in the season:

Blessed art thou, O Lord our God, King of the Universe,
who has kept us in life, and has preserved us,
and has enabled us to reach this season.

Others may be said, for example, on entering a new house, or
wearing new clothes, and on birthdays or other special anniver-
saries. Or this one on seeing deformed persons:

Blessed art thou, O Lord our God, King of the Universe,
who variest the form of thy creatures.

This is a good example of the way in which we might put the most
positive construction on the reality of the created order. Or this
remarkable one, to be said 'on going to stool':

Blessed art thou, O Lord our God, King of the Universe,
who hast made many wonderful orifices in man,
so that if some be opened and others closed
life cannot be sustained.

Something of the same sort of spirituality drawn out of reflection on
the created order can be seen in much of the Celtic tradition, which
has a vogue these days in a rather romanticized form. This house
blessing is an example:

The peace of God, the peace of men,
The peace of Columba kindly,
The peace of Mary mild, the loving,
The peace of Christ, King of tenderness,
    The peace of Christ, King of tenderness;

Be upon each window, upon each door,
Upon each hole that lets in light,
Upon the four corners of my house,
Upon the four corners of my bed,
    Upon the four corners of my bed;

Upon each thing my eye takes in,
Upon each thing my mouth takes in,
Upon my body that is of earth,
And upon my soul that comes from on high,
   Upon my body that is of earth,
   And upon my soul that comes from on high.

('A Gaelic Blessing', from *The Pilgrim Prayerbook*, Continuum, 2003)

Making the sign of the cross as we enter church, dipping our hand in the baptismal water in the font or stoup – or even before we dive beneath the waves when going for a swim – is a sacramental recall of our Baptism. Going to kiss the icons when entering an Orthodox church is to greet our friends and guardians, the saints. They are really present in their icons, which are not just 'representations' in the sense that pictures are in the Western world.

The sacramental sense of presence and place is another important way of marking place and territory as sacred. Sticking a palm cross over the door, like an Orthodox Jew nails a miniature scroll to the doorpost, is a way of hallowing your home. A sense of place, and the desire to mark out or create a temple – a precinct marked out as an orderly space from the surrounding chaos just as Romulus created Rome by driving a ploughshare round the territory within which law and order were to be sustained – is deeply rooted. Even in tidy suburbia, we like to mark out our boundaries with privet hedges and garden gates. This is partly because in crowded and cluttered lives we need to establish our sense of personal space. But there is the obverse: there is also a search for the places in the world which are naturally temple-like, places where people sense the nearness of the other or the transcendent. People have a fine sense for these thin places of the world, like the Islands of Delos in the Aegean or Iona off the west coast of Scotland, islands where the light has that particularly luminous quality shared with many mountaintops, which gives people a sense of the closeness of God. People have built shrines and markers in those spots – little churches to the prophet Elijah on Greek mountaintops or the ruined cells of wild, Celtic saints on inhospitable crags off the west coast of Ireland. But any place can be marked out by the memories of particular experiences: the tree beneath which a young couple pledged their hearts; the spot where you first saw a golden oriole; the church where the shaft of the gospel demand first pierced your self-protective armour; the grave space in which your mother lies buried. Places like that acquire a quasi-sacramental significance because of what happened there to change the pattern of your life and its intertwined relationships.

Funeral rites

People are sometimes surprised to discover that Funeral rites are not sacraments. For much of Christian history, the heart of the Funeral rite was the celebration of the Eucharist: there could be no better way of celebrating the union of the living and the departed in Christ, and of affirming Paul's conviction that 'nothing can separate us from the love of God, which is in Christ Jesus' (Romans 8.39). But the process of saying farewell and the reverent disposal of the body is an important sacramental in that it marks the final stage in a human life. The Christian faith asserts the continuity of our relationship with Christ through death, in spite of the apparent separation that the end of earthly life brings. Though he was writing about the painful separation brought about by deeply held but differing religious convictions, the Puritan Divine, Richard Baxter, makes the point in the verses often sung as a hymn, 'He wants not friends that hath thy love':

> As for my friends they are not lost;
>   The several vessels of thy fleet,
> Though parted now, by tempests toss'd,
>   Shall safely in the haven meet.
>
> Still we are centred all in thee,
>   Members, though distant, of one head;
> In the same family we be,
>   By the same faith and spirit led.
>
> Before thy throne we daily meet
>   As joint-petitioners to thee;
> In spirit we each other greet,
>   And shall again each other see.

> The heavenly hosts, world without end,
>   Shall be my company above;
> And thou, my best and surest Friend,
>   Who shall divide me from thy love?

The rituals that surround death include mourning and grieving, looking forward as well as back. There are other cycles surrounding the rituals of illness, hospitalization and recovery; and around retirement, moving into retirement housing and maybe complete care at the end of life. The Church has an opportunity to accompany people in all these stages with significant opportunities for ritual expression.

Sacramental signs in daily life

But to a Christian, who is always looking for the possibility of contributing to what God is continuing to do in transforming human life, the whole of life is potentially sacramental. Sacramental moments occur naturally in human life: while place and mood are important in creating the opportunity, there is often a vivid moment which focuses our attention and acts as the catalyst. In many such sacramental moments, we are not only challenged but actually offered opportunity for change. This may include formal occasions like people standing round a war memorial (place) on Remembrance Sunday with the leaves all falling off the trees (mood), playing the 'Last Post' (the sharp sound of the bugle acting as the catalyst). Or the experience and wonder of childbirth, which brings us a perception of creative processes which are not ours to control. In spite of the pain and all the palaver, something extraordinary is happening which takes us beyond ourselves. That moment too may offer the sense of participating in God's creative and life-changing activity. Other quasi-sacramental occasions when we are taken out of ourselves and hold our breath include such moments as when people are completely still at the end of the performance of a piece of music, or catch their breath when they come to the crest of a hill and see the view unfold at their feet.

To develop a sense of the sacramental, it is important to remember that God's activity is not controlled by the Church, nor is God experienced there only. In his Gospel, St John highlights water and the spirit as the basic raw elements of creation, and uses them in a way that makes almost everything that Jesus says and does into signals of a new creation. His Gospel is full of signs that take natural processes, like the growth of a vine, and help us to see them as ways of entering imaginatively into the divine life. What is important is that in this new creation by water and the spirit the emphasis is not on the outcome so much as the process. 'Beloved, we are God's children now; it does not yet appear what we shall be, but we know that when he appears we shall be like him, for we shall see him as he is' (1 John 3.2, RSV) is the motto for this developing relationship of transformation.

So the ministry of the Church and the way in which the Church picks up the activities of Christ and formally celebrates them as a community in John's theology is seen as an exercise in both making the new creation visible and in helping to bring it about. Sacraments and sacramental moments and places, therefore, are what unlock opportunities for recognizing the activity of God in the natural order of things.

Artistic creation as sacramental

The other area in which there is a natural sacramentality at work is in the whole field of artistic creation. The artist, whatever he or she thinks that they are doing in painting a picture or composing an opera, sculpting a figure or writing a poem, is essentially drawing people beyond the surface of what they see into an engagement with a story or a thought process or a way of understanding the world, with the hope that the encounter will be fruitful and life-changing.

Artistic creations are not merely decorative objects, they are created signs that point to a reality beyond themselves. Neil McGregor could stand a group in front of a single picture at the National Gallery on Good Friday and help them to a genuinely sacramental encounter. An encounter like this with a work of art is consciously creating a parallel to those 'thin' places like Delos or Iona, where we sense that the seen and unseen worlds are only barely separated, and which offer an almost sacramental experience.

But in many ways, the performing arts like opera and chamber music are richer sacramentally because they have a more obvious quasi-liturgical life of their own. Performances exist in space and time. They can't exist independently of the performers and producers who make them. So although you may read a musical score or read the text of *Hamlet* to yourself or even listen on a disc, when it comes to it, the experience of being in that church listening to that performance of Bach's *St John Passion* or Britten's *Curlew River* is going to be different from standing in front of that Grünewald *Crucifixion* or the Rublev icon by yourself, which is a more private experience for each person. The musical score or the text of a play is a thread which joins performances together, yet each performance is an individual creation, and needs the creative input of the conductor or director and the actors and players to bring it into being.

So whenever the Church sees something that it wants to draw people's attention to and seeks to engage them in it because it reckons that it is part of what God is trying to achieve, it may well want to make the connections with some sacramental kind of celebration. An example might be those acts of corporate reconciliation when whole communities patch up differences and agree to accept one another. It was Archbishop Tutu who presided over the Truth Commission in the new South Africa. And was not the Good Friday Agreement in Northern Ireland, achieved on that day, at least sacramental of the sacrificial and reconciling love of God? The Letter to the Ephesians speaks about the walls of partition being broken down, and it looks very much as though it is the script for this kind of activity, and especially for the dismantling of the Berlin Wall. When politicians or the United Nations think of justifying their work in the public domain, do they think of it as having that sacramental quality? Certainly people like Dag Hammarskjöld, the former Secretary General, thought that it did. He wrote in *Markings*:

> I don't know who – or what – put the question, I don't know when it was put. I don't even remember answering. But at some moment I did answer Yes to Someone – or Something – and from that hour I was certain that existence is meaningful and that, therefore, my life in self-surrender had a goal. From that moment I have known what it means 'not to look back', and 'to take no thought for the morrow'.

And, in the form of a prayer:

> Night is drawing nigh –
> For all that has been – Thanks!
> For all that shall be – Yes!

Recognition

There is no tidy or officially agreed list of sacramentals or sacramental moments in the public domain; they are events or happenings which lead us to recognize and get a glimpse of God's work going on in the world; they are like what Bishop Ian Ramsey called 'disclosure situations' because behind them is a theology of transfiguration. What happens at Jesus' transfiguration on the mountain is a glimpse of how things might be if only . . . This is partly what sacramentals are doing. They are giving us a window into what George Herbert calls 'heaven in ordinarie', or a glimpse of the ordered world, or a glimpse of new life in Christ. If we can glimpse that world often enough and pattern ourselves in this way of seeing, then that world actually becomes not just a wish, a desire or a dream but part of an achievable reality.

Getting into the habit of seeing in this way is like learning to drive a car. You don't, when somebody steps out into the road just in front of you, think 'Now what I need to do is not hit them and therefore what I need to do is stop the car and therefore what I need to do is find the brake pedal, and then I can get my foot on it.' You find yourself doing all that instantaneously and entirely spontaneously because you have learnt to drive the car. In the same way, when you can play the piano properly, a piece of music that you have learnt just falls under your fingers and you don't have to worry about playing it note by note. What you are doing is keeping the architecture of the music and its overall shape in mind.

This is also what happens when you prepare to read a lesson in church. The first stage in getting the meaning into your bones is to set the passage in context, reading what comes before. Then you can understand the shape, not only of the sentence that you are reading, but also by having some picture of where that sentence fits into the whole lesson. It is all part of learning to see how the picture as a whole gives sense to the particular.

Because particular sacramental moments, whether they are encounters with people, artistic experiences or mundane happenings shot through with charged meaning, offer us a glimpse of a world that is essentially sacramental, they give us heightened awareness about our place within the created order, and how that shapes the experience of our life-journey. They alert us to a way of looking at the world which sees a pattern or an order beneath the surface if we have the eyes to see it. This is learning to discern the signs of the kingdom, or in other words to see the connectedness of things, to use relational language.

Our sacramental work

People have high sacramental expectations of doctors and nurses in hospital. They are the people who make it all happen; the patient just lies there and comes out better. That is not to say they effect change magically, though hospitals have a strange mystique, but they make change possible by bringing into relationship a number of strands – the medical, the surgical, the nursing care, the controlled environment, the social and psychological support – that together transform a patient's health. The recognizably transforming encounter may be with the professional doctor or other staff member, or the significant intervention may turn out to be the nurse's engaging with the patient's family circumstances that have contributed to their dis-ease. This is dramatically reflected by the writers of hospital soaps, in which the interest lies not only in the blood and guts and the excitement of the crisis, but also in the drama of human lives and their need for reconciliation. The staff work patiently to bring patients together with their estranged relatives and friends and to restore the relationships which make the patient's life whole again.

There are many work situations where valuable creative contributions are possible, bringing people together in order that change may take place. Isn't that what the teacher is doing by bringing students face to face with opportunities for self-discovery in learning about the world in order that their eyes may be opened? And the sacramental nature of work not only applies to the 'caring' professions, or only to those in the creative professions we have looked at (art, music, drama). In all walks of life people are transforming lives through their daily work. I remember a parish priest in Bristol telling me about his parish: it was a forgotten estate where many people's lives were imprisoned in debt, with consequent collapse of family life. There were high crime levels, and many broken families, and the social services were tearing their hair out. Then a splendid bank manager arrived who transformed the situation by spending his time talking to his clients and helping them to manage their finances. But of course, this didn't make any money for the bank. So what did they do? They closed the branch, and demoted the manager to be an assistant in a plush, suburban branch. Mercifully these days there are credit unions emerging all over the country to help people manage their precarious finances, and these credit unions depend entirely on a network of local relationships within which people are glad to let their tiny surplus savings offer someone a chance of surviving the sudden blip that the collapse of a trusty old banger or a sudden illness has caused.

That kind of situation raises the question as to whether the whole economic structure of our society can be seen as co-operating with the purposes of God, or whether it is about insulating ourselves from any contact with the demands of God or the kind of activities that might be kingdom-building. On a more pragmatic note, helping people to change their lives may require a broader approach than is often allowed for in the settings in which we work. I am thinking particularly of the economic situations of many sub-Saharan countries in Africa. In an understandable attempt to help people to define the goals and purposes of their work, and to be accountable for what they produce, institutions like the World Bank define boundaries and set targets. But this often limits the effectiveness of their intervention – as with the bank manager in Bristol. If his work could have been judged in a wider context – of benefit to the whole community, rather than the narrow one of the bank's financial targets – what he was achieving would have been judged to be a success.

Here again we are looking for a way in which different interests can be drawn together, and the relationship between them built up to transform a situation: this is not just dewy-eyed idealism – there are places where banks sit down with social workers and debt experts and credit unions and agree about how to work together to benefit the community. Jubilee 2000 found ways to work with banks and governments and with international organizations towards the cancellation of the world's unpayable debt. That this is possible in a world driven largely by economic factors is a sign (or sacramental) of the kingdom.

So how do people attend to these signs of the kingdom in their working lives? How do they prepare themselves to see what God is doing in each new day, recognize that it is indeed God's world that they are entering, and find a way of participating in it? Part of the answer lies in whether we actually expect God to be active and wanting our help in building his kingdom, or not. That is where the pattern of daily prayer, with the rhythm of the four Lucan Canticles raising our expectations and helping us to see where we might contribute, is significant, whether we describe it in terms of the angel tapping us on the shoulder or people having their eyes opened to what God is doing and the signs of his kingdom. Daily prayer (see Chapter 5) is enormously important for lay people as well as for clergy.

How do we make this happen?

If we believe that God is at work in the world we have to believe that God knows what to do in order to bring his kingdom into being. We can bring people into conjunction and persuade them to talk to each other but we have to leave the process of transformation to God and let him work in the space that is created. Reconciliation is a gift, not the proper outcome of good management. Creating this space and holding it, is what intercessory prayer is about. Too much of our intercession is about setting out what is wrong with the situation and telling God what we want to happen to transform it. Yet, as the disciples who lived in Emmaus discovered, when we hold together our concern for what is going on in the world with Christ's real presence, known in the breaking of bread, powerful things can happen that we could never foresee.

Moments of change in the Emmaus story

There are two models of the Christian life that chime in with our experience. The first is of our life as a pilgrimage, with Jesus as a companion on the way, guiding us in conversation as he walks the way with us. This is modelled by the sculpture of Christ with his companions on the way to Emmaus in the cloisters of San Domingo de Silos, just off the pilgrim route to Compostela. We know that Christ is leading his companions on the pilgrimage through life, as he is dressed in a woolly hat with a staff in his hand, and his satchel bears the pilgrim badge of the scallop shell on its flap. The model of the pilgrimage is one of a long journey, like the journey through life, in which much change is so gradual as to be hardly visible: a growing teenager seems much the same from one day to the next; but if you've not seen them over the whole of the summer holiday they seem almost unrecognizably different at the end of it. But that model of leisurely companionship, which feels as if it has more to do with development than change, doesn't allow sufficiently for the sharp moments of decision, when we encounter an obstacle and have to decide which way to turn. Some changes are more radical or immediate: a decision to take a new job or to start a family will have far-reaching consequences; and life is never the same again.

But there is another model of encounter with God visible in the Emmaus story as well. This is of encounter with the God who suddenly stands in the way at a narrow point and holds up to us the need for radical change. 'You fools,' says the Christ who walks unrecognized with his companions, 'and slow of heart to believe.' The relationship with God that we long for is not all about sympathetic listening and encouraging each other with stories on the way. There are the moments of decisive challenge too, when we are brought up short. That is what happened to Balaam and his ass (Numbers 22.21–35), when the Angel of God, visible only to the ass, stands in the way and refuses to let Balaam go on without confronting the moment of radical re-orientation which the encounter demands.

Angels

The angel who met Balaam with the drawn sword is the one who stands in the way and says you simply can't go down that route. That is very different from the angel who taps us on the shoulder and invites us to step forward. The angels have this dual role, both of guardianship and of invitation: the angel who steps into Mary's life brings an invitation, and invites an answer. And angels accompany us on the way, as they went with Tobias. Taking the right road is important: turning back on your tracks is not allowed. Look what happened to Lot's wife who turned back for a last look at dear old Sodom, and became a geological specimen.

The sacraments celebrate these radical moments of change in the more orderly pattern of the Christian life. They do not contradict the sense that God accompanies us on the way but rather highlight the moments when we come to a threshold or a choice of direction, and are consciously stepping from one place or mode of life to the next. That is the point to make a sacramental articulation of the change that is taking place which is both about recognizing where we have got to on the journey and about the opportunity that God holds out before us to be conscious of the change, grateful for the opportunity, wanting to celebrate where we have got to, and so find a new direction and the confidence to go forward.

That is why the sense of escaping out of dark, oppressive, confined spaces into a wider one is always important, and that is why the Christian journey can be written as a series of invitations to move forward from one space into the next. 'In my Father's house are many mansions' (John 14.2, AV) and we are held in the embrace of each one for a moment of encounter before the vision of what lies ahead draws us on again. It is a stop–go pattern with moments when we cross the threshold from one room to the next, pausing to centre on a particular encounter with God.

This is what all relationships are like. But what leads us on is always this sense of attention and engagement that leads to transformation and change that is at the heart of every relationship, and especially our relationship with God. It's a relationship that is at the heart of the Christian life, and one that we are always on the verge of losing. When the disciples forsook Jesus as he was arrested in the Garden after that Last Supper, and only the boldest – Peter – dared show his face anywhere where he might be recognized until after the execution, it might have seemed as if that relationship was at an end. After all, death seems pretty final. Little wonder the disciples were dejected as they walked back to Emmaus.

12 | **Lost and Found: The Easter Pattern of Living Now**

What is distinctive about both sacraments and sacramentals is that they make connections and hold things in relationship. It is this pattern of relationships that gives order and meaning to our world.

There are various images of this in the spiritual life. We may talk about being drawn into the life of the Holy Trinity, and picture ourselves before the Rublev icon where the three mysterious figures, waiting for Abraham's breakfast, seem to include us in their company around the table. We may know ourselves drawn into the feast of heaven by the love which has an answer for all our excuses, like George Herbert's 'Love bade me welcome' which ends simply with those six compelling monosyllables 'So I did sit and eat':

> Love bade me welcome: yet my soul drew back,
> > Guiltie of dust and sinne.
> But quick-ey'd Love, observing me grow slack
> > From my first entrance in,
> Drew nearer to me, sweetly questioning,
> > If I lack'd any thing.
>
> A guest, I answer'd, worthy to be here:
> > Love said, you shall be he.
> I the unkinde, ungratefull? Ah my deare,
> > I cannot look on thee.
> Love took my hand, and smiling did reply,
> > Who made the eyes but I?
>
> Truth Lord, but I have marr'd them: let my shame
> > Go where it doth deserve.
> And know you not, sayes Love, who bore the blame?
> > My deare, then I will serve.
> You must sit down, sayes Love, and taste my meat:
> > So I did sit and eat.

Or we may suddenly find ourselves pinned to the spot, like some captured moth, as St Francis was before the vision of the crucified Christ, marked for life by the inescapable and transfiguring wounds; or we may, like St John of the Cross or Catherine of Siena, find ourselves caught up in an ecstatic love affair where we are powerless to resist.

But these are all images. At their heart is the security of a relationship; of knowing and being known in love. This is why the experience of loss, real and permanent loss even of little things, rocks us so badly. If things aren't where they should be, where we know they always are, then the foundations of our ordered world slip. We become disorientated as cosmos descends into chaos.

When I lose something, my first instinct is to blame others for moving it and then enlist them in the search. 'Where did you put the car keys?', 'I left my pen on the hall table; have you taken it?', 'Where's Shakespeare gone? We always keep him on that middle shelf.' And in our household, there's a special tone of voice (mine, I regret to say) reserved for enquiries about the other half of a pair of socks. All in all, a fair proportion of my domestic life is given up to searching for things that I've lost, and the search is often accompanied by thinly veiled accusations that someone else has moved or hidden or taken what I'm looking for.

Some people live such ordered lives that they cannot identify with this at all. For them, the unsettlement I am talking about may be more like walking in to your home, and finding that the grandfather clock that has always greeted you by the staircase just isn't there: it's gone – stolen, and never to return.

The sense of loss, even in little things, is deeply disorientating, and leads us to flail around, accusing others of messing up our lives. So how much more when the loss is not the loss of a pen or a book, but of the person you love – of the only significant person in your life. That's what happens when the person you love dies, and when any important relationship is abruptly ended. That is what happened to the disciples, and it's because Mary Magdalene's sense of loss seems so devastating that her story of being lost and found remains at the nucleus of the good news of Easter.

When Mary goes early to the tomb where Jesus had been hastily buried, she finds the stone rolled away. She goes for help, and Peter and John come running: there's nothing there that they can see except the grave clothes. Has the grave been desecrated?

When Mary dares to face the emptiness – the fact that the body, the only tangible contact with the new life she had glimpsed in Jesus, is gone – she is helped to put her fears into words: 'Why are you weeping?' 'Because they have taken away my Lord, and I do not know where they have laid him.' Not knowing what has happened, not having the body, not having a place – a known place – where the body is laid to rest is deeply troubling. When you can no longer see or hear the person you love, and the other senses have gone, graves are important. You can still touch the spot, and feel some contact with the one who has died; we put fresh flowers on graves years after the death of the one who lies there.

So Mary, raw with the sense of loss both of person and of place, turns from peering into the blackness of the cave and sees a figure silhouetted against the light that she assumes is the gardener. Through her tears, she asks him where he has taken the body. All he says is 'Mary', and she knows.

The name – her name – sounds magical. It's that way of saying her name that restores in an instant the fragile relationship that she had thought was severed for ever. It's that quality of personal rela-tionship – knowing and being known by name – that matters. The person who knows those who work for them by name is the one who commands loyalty. It's that quality of relationship – of knowing and being known – that those who are baptized and con-firmed in the dawn of Easter Day have discovered for themselves. In the middle of the griefs and miseries of a selfish world, where people are out to grab what they can for themselves and throw their weight around to achieve it, it's knowing God, and knowing that you are known by him, that counts.

And we are not here talking about the kind of propositional certainty that Thomas wanted. We are not talking about proof, or facts, or knowledge. We are talking about knowing and being known personally; about relationships.

Sometimes the liturgy we inherit does not help us to see that. Early in the dawn of Easter Day I find myself asking the congrega-tion to join with the candidates in saying the Apostles' Creed. They duly rehearse their faith in the time-honoured phrases, used by can-didates at the brink of the waters of baptism since the early days of the Church. The propositions in that baptismal creed have stood the test of time, and are what is called the *Symbolum Fidei*, the symbol or standard of the faith. The formal propositions in the creeds do not build up an identikit photograph, a literal picture of God; they are more like a coat of arms, or a flag – something that we can identify with, something to which we can pledge our allegiance, and which we can recognize across the ages.

The creeds have indeed served us well in keeping the Church united in its allegiance to God the Holy Trinity over the centuries, yet the truth about God – about Christ's dying and rising for us – is essentially personal, not propositional. You can't fall in love with a form of words; but you can with a person. And, like Mary Magdalene, we have and we do.

That's why the touchstone of the personal name is so vital. In Isaiah (43.1–2, RSV) God says to his people:

> Fear not, for I have redeemed you;
>   I have called you by name, you are mine.
> When you pass through the waters I will be with you;
>   and through the rivers, they shall not overwhelm you;
> when you walk through fire you shall not be burned,
>   and the flame shall not consume you.

Isaiah could be describing the journey of baptism, as well as the journey of the people of Israel; indeed, he could well be foretelling the Dawn Liturgy in Salisbury Cathedral. But he could as well be describing the way God stands with us when we are confronted with the loss of someone we love. When the risen Christ called Mary by name in the garden, she knew that death had not severed their relationship.

> My beloved is mine, and I am his, . . .
> Many waters cannot quench love,
> neither can floods drown it.

says the writer of the Song of Songs (2.16, 8.7, RSV).

But such a love song hardly does justice to the pain that comes with sharing in Christ's suffering for his world. The hands of the risen Christ, lifted in blessing, are scarred with the wounds of the nails. The one who stands among the seven golden lampstands and ever lives to make intercession for us is the one within whose wounded side we are drawn:

> Within your wounds hide me
> and suffer me never to be separated from Thee

prays the traditional prayer at the moment of receiving the sacrament; it is the wounded Christ that we hold in our hands in the broken bread of communion. It is within the broken body that we are enfolded in love.

So our union with the risen Christ unites us with the world's pain; the pain of the peoples of Iraq, and the Sudan and Jerusalem; the pains of the sick, the injured and the dying; the pain of all who know separation, loss and bereavement.

That is why, in a haunting phrase, echoing Janet Morley:

> I will cry for my beloved and will not rest
> Until I dwell in the darkness of his embrace
> And all my silence is enclosed in him.

Is God calling you by name? The proof of the resurrection is not to be found in gazing into the abyss of the empty tomb, but in the risen Christ meeting you on the way and, like Mary in the Garden, calling you by name. The proof of the resurrection is not a statement or an assertion: it is knowing yourself, like Mary, to be called by name, and loved by God with a love that will never let you go.

And that's the discovery I wish for you.

And the pattern for the Church?

We are at the end of an era. The Church of the future will continue to have institutional expression and an ordered life. There will be a means of recognizing Christian belief and practice in different cells of the Church's life – a pattern of communion within which we can accept one another as fellow Christians. But the Church's life – its vitality – will not be discovered primarily in institutional allegiance or in an individual's spiritual journey. It will be discovered in relationships; our individual relationship with the God who calls us by name, and our relationships with one another.

It is in small groups that relationships can develop those bonds of trust where reconciliation is earthed. It is in small groups that people learn to pray and read the Scriptures together. That is where we learn how to engage our faith with how to live as a responsible human being. That is where we gain the confidence to interpret what God is saying to us and can be encouraged to respond to his call.

In this process of growing up spiritually and supporting one another, the Church has a crucial function. The Church holds together the past, the present and the future and weaves us into that continuing pattern. That's what tradition means: the process of handing on the faith from person to person. In the past, the Church has been understood as existing primarily in its various institutional forms, given shape by its publicly recognized ministries and holding a body of unchanging doctrines. For many people who are church-goers, the Church is 'them' – the clergy, the bishops, the dioceses, the official bodies. But the Church is not 'them'; it is 'us'. This is the kind of being Church that will nurture people's excitement and help us grow in confidence and holiness.

In many ways, the Church of England is well equipped to respond to this future. Our historic practice has led us to understand the Church less in terms of an authoritative structure with a hier-archical chain of command and more in terms of a raft that supports people in their journey. In the Church of England, worship is inter-leaved with learning, leadership merges with companionship, and the Church is there to keep people afloat, travelling in the same direction and glad of each other's insights as well as company.

Historically, many churches have placed great weight on a linear process of transmission. They see the Church as an edifice, linked to its past by an unbroken chain of clearly forged doctrinal links, each dependent on those that went before. The danger here is that if just one link snaps, the whole edifice collapses. The Church of England on the other hand has seemed more like a raft or hammock, where the many threads, none of them particularly strong in themselves, are tightly woven together to take the strain. Even if the hammock seems to be largely holes, it is capable of sustaining heavy weights and can cope with several of the strands fraying or breaking without the whole bundle crashing to the ground.

Behind these basic convictions lies a pattern that undergirds the way this book has taken shape. The pattern is found in Scripture and tradition, and it appeals to reason – or at least to common sense – too. It is anchored scripturally in the narrative of the journey to Emmaus in Luke 24 and is unfolded in every celebration of the Eucharist.

This pattern that we absorb into our lifeblood – this repetitive spiral of attending, engaging, transforming and being energized to move out again – strikes a chord with basic common sense: it looks as if God's way of doing things is basically a natural one, if only we could learn it. To change things, we must engage; if we are to engage with people, we must first attend to them. And change delivers us back at the start of the cycle, ready to attend all over again.

That is why this has essentially been a circular journey, but one which I hope has drawn you further into the heart and purposes of a God who is always going before us. As we pray:

> Prevent us, O Lord, in all our doings with thy most gracious favour, and further us with thy continual help; that in all our works, begun, continued, and ended in thee, we may glorify thy holy name, and finally by thy mercy obtain everlasting life; through Jesus Christ our Lord. Amen.
>
> (Collect in the Eucharist, Book of Common Prayer)

Or in the words of the Psalmist:

> Yet I am always with you;
> you hold me by my right hand.
>
> You will guide me with your counsel
> and afterwards receive me with glory.
>
> Whom have I in heaven but you?
> And there is nothing upon earth that I desire
> in comparison with you.
>
> Though my flesh and my heart fail me,
> God is the strength of my heart and my portion for ever.
>
> (Psalm 73.23–26, *Common Worship*)

That is more like the language of love, of an intimate relationship, that not even death can sever.